Learn the Symbols and Terms That Can Keep You Ahead in the Investment Game!

...ON THE STOCK EXCHANGE—Find out what listing can tip you off to a highly profitable share purchase...and the column figure that can be your clue to finding progressive—and potentially profitable—companies.

...ON THE MONEY MARKET—Learn the symbol that tells you what funds are exempt from income tax...and why a short portfolio maturity figure is best.

...AND IN HIGH-RISK COMMODITIES FUTURES— Discover how to tell which product futures are the most liquid...and how the smallest change in their figures can mean major profits...

All this and more in the book that translates the mumbo-jumbo of the financial world into useful, profit-making information...

★★★

HOW TO READ THE FINANCIAL PAGES

Also by Peter Passell

Personalized Money Strategies
Where to Put Your Money
Where to Put Your Money 1985
Where to Put Your Money 1986
Where to Put Your Money 1987

Published by
WARNER BOOKS

PETER PASSELL

HOW TO READ THE FINANCIAL PAGES

(Revised Edition)

WARNER BOOKS

A Time Warner Company

WARNER BOOKS EDITION

Cover design by Diane Luger

Warner Books, Inc.
1271 Avenue of the Americas
New York, N.Y. 10020

A Time Warner Company

Printed in the United States of America

First Printing: March, 1993

10 9 8 7 6 5 4 3 2 1

Contents

Introduction

Millions of Americans own stocks, bonds, mutual funds, commodity futures, options, and a dozen hybrid securities traded each day on the nation's exchanges. Millions more, who belong to pension plans or own life insurance, have an indirect stake in what is happening on the money markets. But cruzeiros to croissants, not one investor in a hundred knows what the little d after the price of a listed stock means, why the S & P 500 Index sometimes goes down while the Dow-Jones Industrial Average is going up, or why Wall Street goes bananas whenever the Federal Reserve announces a new target for something called "M2."

There has always been a way to find out, of course. An afternoon at the public library or an investment in $50 worth of stock market tomes does the trick. But it's hard and not always rewarding work, almost as painful as studying for your Econ 101 midterm in college, or having lunch with your tax accountant.

Enter *How To Read the Financial Pages*, a very short,

very understandable, very affordable guide that delivers just what it says.

Part One: THE TABLES translates the daily financial listings into plain English and adds some tips on how to read between the lines. Stocks and bonds come first. But the fancier stuff—index options, commodity futures, and foreign exchange—are included, too.

Part Two: THE NUMBERS explains what commonly cited statistics ranging from the Over-the-Counter Stock Index, to the weekly money supply figures, to the Producer Price Index really mean and how they may affect your investments.

Read it straight through in a few hours, or just keep it around as a reference. *How To Read the Financial Pages* doesn't provide the names of twenty-one stocks guaranteed to double in twenty-one months. It won't even make you the life of the party. But it certainly does offer an easy-to-read key to the financial information you must have to stay ahead of the game.

Getting Started

You can't tell the players—or in this case, the payers—without a scorecard. But which scorecard?

Thanks to increased interest on the part of readers (not to mention fear of losing their audience to television), newspapers in larger cities have improved their coverage of business events. The basic securities market tables look pretty much the same, no matter where you read them. That's because all newspapers print the same data compiled by the same computers and transmitted by the same wire services. *For many investors the tables, financial data, and general economics reporting in their daily morning papers will provide all they need to keep up.*

In fact, the very best papers, such as the *Boston Globe*, *Los Angeles Times*, *Miami Herald*, and *Milwaukee Journal*, offer something the national dailies can't: local business news. If you hunger for more, though, try one of these:

The *Wall Street Journal*. The most complete and accurate coverage of business news to be found, the *Journal* doesn't have any real competitors. In spite of recent scandals, its "Heard on the Street" report remains the most influential column on the stock market. The only drawback to the *Journal* is its bulk. Sixty to seventy pages of business and economics can be a time-consuming and—dare it be mentioned—boring way to start the day.

Edited in New York but printed in a dozen places around the world, the *Wall Street Journal* can be ordered for same-day home delivery in most parts of the country.

The *Financial Times*. Though unfamiliar to most American readers, the London-edited *Financial Times* is a sort of *Wall Street Journal* for English-speaking Europeans. The big advantage is that it covers European and third-world business news in much greater detail. This can be quite useful for investors who want to buy foreign securities. The small advantage is that it reports American business news with detachment, never overemphasizing the importance of events simply because they happened in America.

The *New York Times*. Its first-rate daily business section represents a compromise between the exhaustive coverage of the *Wall Street Journal* and the once-over-lightly-courtesy-of-the-Associated-Press coverage offered by the average daily newspaper. Some people subscribe to the *Wall Street Journal* for weekday coverage and then buy the *Times* on Sunday. Its Sunday business section is full of ads for new investment products, as well as magazine-type stories on trends in business and economics.

USA Today. Built around the concept that "less is more," the national newspaper published by the Gannett chain covers a lot of business and financial news in a compact space. Its daily Money section, packed with multicolored charts and 3-D graphs, is easy to read and jargon free. The one big disadvantage: very limited securities listings. Those who follow options, futures, and bonds will have to look elsewhere.

Investors Daily. This relatively new daily newspaper is trying to secure a very special niche for itself. Unlike the *Journal* or the *New York Times*, it makes little effort to cover broad economic or financial news. The emphasis is on the detailed tables and data needed by professional investors. If, for example, you want a breakdown on hour-to-hour trading for the most actively traded stocks of the previous day, the only place to get it is in *Investors Daily.* It is available in big cities, but newsstand distribution elsewhere is thin.

Barron's. An immensely influential weekly newspaper for investors, published by the Dow Jones Company in tabloid form. Once narrowly aimed at professionals, it has livened up its reporting and broadened its coverage to make it more interesting to the serious amateur. Barron's compilation of tables is the most comprehensive available. It is particularly useful to investors who follow small "over-the-counter" stocks that are not regularly reported in the dailies.

PART ONE

The Tables

New York and American Stock Exchange Composite Transactions

The stocks of most large, publicly owned corporations are traded on either the New York or the American Stock Exchange. There is more status in being listed on the New York Exchange. The minimum requirements for the total value of outstanding shares and the total number of stockholders are somewhat stricter. But from the perspective of the stock buyer, there is hardly any difference.

Both exchanges have fancy computer systems for executing orders and assuring that all customers are treated equally. Both exchanges do a pretty good job of policing brokers to keep them honest. Both report transactions the same way, so if you understand how to read the stock tables for one, you automatically understand the other.

The stock tables in morning newspapers are based on all the trading activity for the previous day. Afternoon newspapers sometimes limit their reports to what has

PETER PASSELL

happened up to noon or 2 p.m. *Either way, the figures reported are composite transactions. If a stock is listed on more than one exchange—say, the New York and a regional stock exchange like the Pacific—the table automatically includes all transactions.*

Column 1. The highest price paid for EGG (the E.G.&G. Company, a manufacturer of electronics components located in Massachusetts) over the past 52 weeks

EXCHANGE STOCKS*

	1		2	3	4
52 WEEKS					YLD
HIGH	LOW	STOCK	DIV		&
2½	¾	Digicn wt	. .		. .
40	26⅛	EGG	.48		1.3
31⅝	21¼	E-Syst	.50		1.8
30⅞	20½	Echlin	.88e		3.3
19	16⅛	ElcAut n	. .		. .
38	27-14	Enron s	1.30		3.8
47	43	Ensch pf	4.18		9.5
1	9/32	vjFairfd	. .		. .

*Transaction information for illustration only.

4

was $40 a share. The lowest price was $26.125. Most listed stocks, by the way, are priced in eighths of a dollar. When issues are trading at very low prices, though, prices are sometimes shown in sixteenths or even thirty seconds.

Column 2. Stock names are abbreviated by the Associated Press wire service in order to fit the space in

5	6	7		8	9
P-E ratio	Sales 100s	HIGH	LOW	CLOSE	CHG.
. .	7	$1\frac{7}{8}$	$1\frac{3}{4}$	$1\frac{7}{8}$	$+\frac{1}{8}$
20	x219	38	$37\frac{1}{2}$	$37\frac{3}{4}$	$+\frac{1}{4}$
14	156	$28\frac{1}{2}$	28	$28\frac{1}{8}$	$-\frac{3}{8}$
12	111	$27\frac{1}{4}$	$26\frac{7}{8}$	27	$+\frac{1}{4}$
26	559	18	$17\frac{3}{8}$	$17\frac{3}{8}$	$-\frac{3}{8}$
16	1945	$34\frac{7}{8}$	$34\frac{1}{4}$	$34\frac{1}{2}$	$-\frac{5}{8}$
. .	z3900	44	44	44	. .
. .	120	$\frac{7}{16}$	$\frac{3}{8}$	$\frac{13}{32}$	$+\frac{1}{32}$

newspapers. Usually the abbreviation is obvious: "E Syst'" (E-Systems). Sometimes it isn't: "Ensch" (Enserch Company, a conglomerate that owns pipelines and energy interests). But this is rarely a problem because readers of the stock tables are looking for data on specific stocks (whose abbreviations are usually familiar), not browsing the listings.

Most issues listed on the New York and American stock exchanges are "common" stocks, representing basic ownership of the company. Someone who owns, say, 1.338 percent of the outstanding common stock is usually entitled to 1.338 percent of the votes on important company matters and is always entitled to 1.338 percent of the profits. But two other types of securities are also listed on the stock exchanges.

Consider "Digicon wt", the first listing. It is a "warrant," the right to buy a specified number of shares of Digicon stock at a specified price until a specified expiration date. Warrants are often included with an issue of new stock in order to sweeten the deal; you buy 100 shares now for $5 a share, and we'll toss in the right to buy a hundred more at $10 a share any time in the next three years. Once issued, warrants can be bought or sold separately from the stock. *The advantage of buying warrants, as opposed to the underlying stock, is that they are usually highly "levered." If the stock goes up, the warrant will go up even more. Leverage, alas, works both ways: if a stock falls in value, the warrant will fall even more.*

Check out "Ensch pf", the seventh listing. The *pf*

stands for "preferred stock." Preferred stock is a cross between a stock and a bond. Owners of preferred stock, like owners of bonds, are entitled to a specified payment—say $5 a year—before any payment can be made to the owners of the common stock. But unlike the interest on a bond, dividends on preferred stock are not a legal obligation of the company. If a bondholder isn't paid, he has the right to force the company into bankruptcy to collect on the debt. *The claims of preferred stockholders only begin where the creditors' claims end.*

Two other symbols: the letter *n* after the company name (as in "ElcAut n", the fifth listing) means the stock has been issued sometime in the past 52 weeks. In such cases the high and low prices refer to the high and lows since trading in the stock began.

The letters *vj* before the stock name in the bottom row (vjFairfd, the Fairfield Corp.) mean the company is in bankruptcy proceedings.

Why would a stock still be traded if the company were bankrupt? If the company has ceased operations, buyers are betting that the liquidated value of the assets will exceed the price they paid. If the company is unable to pay its creditors but is still operating under the protection of a court, buyers are betting the company will get back on its feet.

Column 3. "Div." stands for dividend, the amount paid to stockholders on an annual basis. E-Systems Company, the second listing, paid a dividend of 12½ cents in the last quarter, equivalent to 50 cents a year.

Some corporations pay dividends on an irregular basis. When followed by an *e* (as in Echlin's .88e), the listed sum is the amount paid over the past year.

Other symbols worth noting:

☞ An *s* (as in "Enron s") means the corporation has issued a dividend in the form of more stock sometime in the past year. For example, a company might give two shares of stock to every holder of three shares. Thus everybody who used to own 300 shares would automatically own 500.

The new 500 shares represent exactly the same fractional ownership of the company as the old 300, and there is every reason to believe that the new, "diluted" shares will be worth only three-fifths as much. So why would a company bother? Occasionally, because the company believes that the high price of the stock has discouraged potential buyers who don't have enough cash to purchase a "round lot" of 100 shares. But usually it is an act of showmanship. The company can't, or doesn't want to, pay out a cash dividend. So to keep the suckers happy, it passes out some extra paper and calls it a dividend.

☞ the letter *g* would mean the dividend is paid in Canadian currency. Some Canadian company stocks are listed on U.S. exchanges and thus traded in U.S. dollars. But dividend checks are Canadian money, whose value fluctuates with the exchange rate between the two currencies.

Column 4. "Yld.%" stands for yield: the current annual dividend divided by the closing price of the stock, expressed as a percentage.

E-System's 50-cent dividend, divided by the closing price, 28⅛, works out to 1.8 percent. When no dividend is paid, as is the case for Fairfield, no yield figure is shown. Nor, by the way, is a yield shown for stocks that pay dividends in Canadian dollars; dividing one currency by another would be misleading.

The yield on a stock looks like the interest on a fixed return security, such as a bond. For preferred stocks, or stocks with stable dividends that pay out most of their earnings, the analogy makes sense. Such stocks fluctuate up and down with interest rates and bond prices.

Low yields don't necessarily mean that a stock is a bad buy. Some of the best-managed companies have a policy of paying out very little in dividends. In some cases that's because the company puts growth financed through retained earnings ahead of other objectives. In others, the policy is calculated to serve the interest of high-tax-bracket stockholders. Retained earnings are taxed as corporate profits. Once paid out as dividends, they are taxed a second time as personal income to the recipient. The second whack can make a big difference to the owner of the stock.

Column 5. The P-E (price-earnings) ratio is the closing price of the stock divided by the company's earnings per share over last 12 months. Thus a stock with a P-E of 9 is selling for roughly nine times last year's after-tax profit per share. No P-E is shown for stocks with no profit or a negative profit. Nor is a P-E ratio shown for preferred stocks, since ownership provides no direct claim on the company's profits.

Probably no single statistic is more informative than the P-E ratio. When a stock has a high P-E, the market anticipates that the earnings of the company will grow rapidly. By the same token, a low P-E reflects the market's view that profits are flat or falling.

Well, that's one theory, anyway. In practice, enthusiasm for a stock may or may not reflect a rational calculation of the company's earnings prospects. Lots of buyers work on the Greater Fool theory: a stock is worth whatever the next fool will pay for it.

Column 6. The Sales column shows the number of shares traded, divided by 100. For example, 15,600 E-Systems shares are sold that day. The letter z in front of a sales number means the figure is the volume in full. Thus z3,900 for Enserch preferred means that 3,900 shares changed hands, not 390,000.

Volume figures are useful for a number of reasons. To begin, the number tells you how liquid the stock is, that is, how easy it is to buy (or sell) the stock without paying more (or selling for less) than the current market price. For example, it is unlikely that an attempt to purchase 2,000 shares of EGG stock would affect a market in which 21,900 shares changed hands the previous day. On the other hand, should you try to purchase 2,000 shares of Enserch preferred when only 3,900 traded the day before, you might well have to pay an extra 50 cents a share.

Volume figures also tell you if something unusual is happening to a stock. For example, if sales were 10 times above average for a few days in a row, it's quite likely that the market is responding to rumors of important news affecting earnings, etc.

One other symbol to remember: the letter *x* in front of volume number (as in EGG's x219) signifies the stock is selling "ex-dividend." That means the seller, not the buyer, is entitled to the most recently declared dividend. This might not matter very much for a stock like EGG that sells for $37 a share and pays just 12 cents quarterly. But for companies that pay high dividends—for example, electric utility shares—a single quarterly dividend can amount to 2 or 3 percent of the stock purchase price.

Column 7. The "High" is the highest price at which the stock changed hands that day. The "Low" is the lowest price. A letter *u* in front of the High means this is the highest price at which the stock has traded in a year. A letter *d* in front of the Low means it is the lowest price the stock has traded in a year. The *Wall Street Journal* uses a different notation. Stocks closing at new highs or lows for the year have little arrows (pointing up or down) in front of column one. Note, too, that the *Wall Street Journal* also puts the n (new issue), x (ex-dividend) and s (stock dividend) symbols in front of column one.

A large difference between the daily High and Low— say, more than 3 or 4 percent of the stock price—usually means one of two things: It is possible that investors have changed their minds about the value of a stock and it has moved sharply up or down. Or, a big spread might simply indicate that the stock is thinly traded. With few buyers and few sellers in the market, trades may take place over a broad range of prices.

Column 8. The "Close" is the last price at which the stock changed hands that day. Remember, by the way, that a seller receives less than the trade price and a buyer pays more. The difference is the commission charged by the brokers, plus any tax collected on the transaction.

Column 9. The "Chg." is the change in the closing price from the previous day.

At the tail end of the American Stock Exchange allowed those up to one-half listed on the small board could be considered with their Regional Options Exchange securities on the NYSE could be handled within the two hours.

American Stock Exchange Emerging Issues

At the tail end of the American Stock Exchange listings are a few dozen stocks separately listed as "Amex Emerging Issues". These are stocks that do not meet the Amex's regular minimum qualifications for listing—in particular, a pre-tax annual income of $750,000 and a minimum share price of $3 at the time of initial listing.

Why, then, has the Amex decided to make special room for these stocks?

Glad you asked. The Amex says it is trying to give a boost to medium-sized companies with good growth potential. Others think it has more to do with the Amex's quest for new business at a time when competition between the exchanges is especially fierce.

Whatever the reason, it makes sense to be a bit wary of these stocks—especially if a brokerage house salesman whom you've never met calls with a hot tip on one of them. They are all lightly traded issues of companies with less than established earnings records, and are thus susceptible to price manipulation by unscrupulous brokers.

NASDAQ Over-the-Counter National Market Issues

Publicly owned companies that can't or don't want to meet the size and disclosure requirements of the New York, American, or regional exchanges are traded "over the counter." The over-the-counter market isn't a physical place like the other stock exchanges. It is a network of brokers who belong to the National Association of Securities Dealers and "make markets" the way specialists do on the floor of the organized stock exchanges—that is, they buy selected stocks when there are no other buyers.

A few decades ago the network operated very informally, depending on mimeographed sheets of buy and sell offers that were produced after trading hours and distributed to dealers the next morning. The actual trading was done by the telephone. Since the 1970s, though, over-the-counter dealers have been tied together by an automated quotation computer system, known as NASDAQ. Trading itself is not automated; that still depends on brokers talking to each other on the telephone. But each broker now has a computer terminal on his or her desk that shows the highest bid price and lowest asking price in the system for several thousand stocks.

Of the 30,000 stocks available over the counter, figures for roughly 1,500 of the most actively traded are reported daily as NASDAQ National Market Issues. In most papers, NASDAQ National market Issues are now identical to the listings for the American and New York Exchanges.

A supplementary list of a few hundred lightly traded NASDAQ stocks is often printed, too. But, here, the tables contain only the highest bid and lowest sale offer, and sometimes the volume of sales.

The *Wall Street Journal* has expanded its NASDAQ National market Issue listings to include the four-letter shorthand for the stock's name, used in the NASDAQ computers. In some cases, there is a fifth letter attached to the symbol which defines special conditions or restrictions on the listed security.

For example, COGN stands for the Cognos Corporation. But the listing shows it as COGNF, with the F showing it is a foreign corporation. Here's a list of the most frequently used fifth letters:

A or B. The class of stock. Some companies issue two classes of common stock, whose owners have, say, different rights to elect corporate directors or restrictions on who may own the shares. Make sure you know what these differences are before you buy.

C. Temporarily exempted from NASDAQ listing qualifications. Unlike the New York and American Stock
Exchanges, the NASDAQ is not fussy about minimum
assets or profits when companies apply for listing. Don't
even consider buying a company that has yet to meet the
minimum unless you know why.

E. Delinquent in legal filings required by the government for public sale on any exchange. What goes for C,
goes double for E.

F. A foreign corporation, one that operates under the
rules of another government. Such companies are still
obliged to meet minimum disclosure requirements set by
the Securities and Exchange commission.

G. Convertible Bond. Like any bond, a convertible
bond obliges the issuer to pay interest on terms set down
in the agreement. Unlike ordinary bonds, however, convertibles may be exchanged for stock at a specified
conversion rate—say, one bond for 27 shares. This gives
the owner the best of both worlds: a guaranteed annual
return (provided the company remains solvent) plus a
chance to participate in the gain in the stock value rises.
Of course, you pay for what you get: Convertibles pay
lower rates of interest than ordinary bonds.

K. Non-Voting Stock. These shares do not carry the
right to elect corporate directors. Companies issue them
in order to raise capital without risking loss of control of
the business to outsiders. Others things being equal, they
aren't as valuable as voting shares.

P. Preferred Stock. A preferred stock is a cross between a stock and a bond. Unlike bond owners, owners

are not legally entitled to a specified annual payment. And unlike common stock owners, they do not have the right to vote for corporate boards. But preferred stock owners must be paid specified dividends before the common stock owners are handed a single penny. And typically, this obligation is cumulative: If the company fails to pay the preferred dividend for six years running, they must pay a full six years' worth of preferred dividends before issuing a common stock dividend.

Q. In bankruptcy proceedings. Stocks trade even after the company goes bankrupt because buyers speculate that the company will be worth something even after the creditors are paid off. This is dangerous territory for amateurs: look before you leap.

R. Rights. When companies decide to issue new shares, they often give existing shareholders the right to buy the shares for a brief period—a month or so—at a specified price. If this price is below the market value, the rights have a value in themselves. Rights are generally freely tradable.

V. When issued. Securities are sometimes bought and sold before they are issued. A company might, for example, announce that it is issuing a stock dividend. Those who expect to receive the new shares can sell them immediately, eliminating the risk that the stock price will fall in the meantime.

W. Warrants. Like rights, warrants entitle the holders to purchase shares at a specified price. Warrants, however, are entitlements that last for years—or even indefinitely. They usually are thrown in as a sweetener when companies issue new bonds or preferred stock.

Y. American Depository Receipt. These are stocks in every sense but the legal sense. They are receipts proving the stock is in the custody of an American bank: the owner of the receipt is legally entitled to any dividends, or any other benefit granted to the stockholder by the company. Why the rigamirole? It is a way for foreign companies to trade their stock on U.S. exchanges without meeting the onerous disclosure requirements of the U.S. securities laws.

New York and American Exchange Bonds

The two big exchanges in New York City make a market for bonds as well as stocks. Most of these bonds (in jargon, "debentures") are the debts of large corporations. But the New York Bond Exchange also carries a few listings for bonds issued by foreign governments.

Trading in bonds is not a game recommended for casual investors. Bonds are contracts written by the borrower. And often these contracts, which spell out in detail the corporate borrower's obligations to the bond owners, are quite complicated.

For example, one has to know more than the creditworthiness of a company to judge the creditworthiness of its bonds. Some bonds are "junior" debt: in the event the company is unable to meet its obligations, the owners of such bonds must wait until other creditors are paid off. Other bonds are "equipment trust certificates," in effect, mortgages on, say, a specific airplane or factory complex owned by the borrower. With equipment trusts, the security of your bond depends less on the credit of the borrower than on the market value of the equipment pledged as collateral.

Many bonds, moreover, contain "call" provisions which allow the borrower to buy back the bonds at a specified price long before maturity. Such provisions work entirely in the borrower's favor. If interest rates in the economy go down, the borrower can redeem the bonds and borrow the money elsewhere at a lower rate. But if interest rates rise, the borrower is under no obligation to redeem the bonds before the maturity. The lender is thus stuck with below-market interest.

The bottom line: Never buy a bond unless you know what you are buying. The only way to be sure what's in the bond contact is to read the prospectus published when the bond was first issued. Any broker worth his commission will be happy to supply you with a copy.

Column 1. A bond is identified by the company that issued it, the interest it pays, and the year in which it matures. Thus "Exxon 6½ 98" is shorthand for a bond issued by the John Deere Corporation that pays 6.5 percent interest ($65 a year) on the $1,000 face value of the bond and matures sometime in 1998. All this information is provided to identify the bond because a company may have more than one bond issue outstanding. "DetEd 9.15s00" is a Detroit Edison Corp. bond paying 9.15 percent interest ($91.50) annually that matures in the year 2000. Interest on most bonds is paid in semiannual installments. Thus owners of the DetEd9.15s00 expect $45.75 every six months.

The maturity date tells you the year in which the bond must be redeemed by the issuing company at the original $1,000 face value. It is possible—no, likely—that the bond contains a call provision giving the company the option to redeem the bond years earlier. The only way to find out is to read the bond prospectus or consult a research service that keeps track of bonds.

"CATS zr06-11" is not a corporate bond at all, but a "Certificate of Accrual on Treasury Securities." This is an obligation of a big bond dealer to pay the holder $1,000 on the maturity date. What makes the obligation special is that it is backed by a U.S. government bond of equal value. Notice the zr; that means this is a zero coupon bond paying no current interest. The profit to the investor is the difference between what he or she pays for the CATS today and their guaranteed value on redemption. This particular CATS has two dates listed, rather than just one. That means it may be redeemed as early as 2006 or as late as 2011.

The t in "Citicp 6.5s98t" means that the interest payment of this Citicorp bond floats—that is, it is adjusted periodically according to some formula that reflects movements in current interest rates. *The advantage of a floating rate security is that the price won't fluctuate very much as interest rates change*. The disadvantage is that you pay for the lower risk: floating-rate bonds pay lower interest than the fixed-rate bonds of equivalently creditworthy borrowers.

Column 2. The current yield is the annual interest the company promises to pay, divided by the last price at which the bond was sold (see column 5).

All bonds are issued in $1,000 denominations. But, just to confuse things, bond prices are listed as a percentage of the $1,000 face value rather than in dollars. Thus the closing price of the Citicorp bond is 91⅛ percent of $1,000, or $911.25. To obtain the current yield of the Citicorp bond, divide the interest payment $65 by the

(TABLE 2)

EXCHANGE BONDS*

	1	2	3
BONDS		**CUR YLD**	**VOL**
AshO	6¾ 14	cv	2
CATS	zr06-11	..	35
Citicp	6.5s98t	7.1	11
DetEd	9.15s00	9.0	5
Exxon	6½ 98	6.8	26

*Transaction information for illustration only

closing price of $911.25. That equals 7.13. To save space in the listings, the figure is rounded to the nearest tenth—7.1.

There is no current yield for AshO (Ashland Oil); instead there is only a cv. The cv means the bond is convertible into a specified number of shares of stock in Ashland Oil.

It would be easy enough to calculate a current yield for the Ashland Oil convertible ($67.50 divided by $892.50

	4		5		6
	HIGH	LOW	CLOSE		NET CHG
	90	89	89¼		-¾
	17	16¾	17		..
	91⅛	91	91⅛		+⅛
	102	101½	102		..
	95¾	95	95½		-¼

equals 7.6 percent). But the number is not printed in the listings because the price of convertible bonds is partially determined by the price of the stock and the terms of the conversion.

Column 3. The volume is the number of bonds that traded hands that day. For example, 26 of the Exxon bonds were traded.

Consider how small this figure is. Exxon is the largest oil company in the world. Yet just $26,000 worth of this bond issue traded on this day. Exxon does have other bonds outstanding, paying different interest rates and maturing at other dates. But even if you include them, the value of bonds traded daily is minuscule compared to the hundreds of millions of dollars worth of Exxon stock that changes hands each day.

The Exxon example is not unusual. Most bonds are purchased by big institutions—pension funds, insurance companies—and either held to maturity or sold in very large blocks in transactions off the exchange. Total trading on the New York Bond Exchange that day was less than $30 million. Compare that to total trading on the New York Stock Exchange, which exceeded $2 billion.

Low volumes matter to individual investors because they make corporate bonds relatively illiquid. If, for example, you tried to sell fifty Exxon bonds on a single day, you might end up receiving $10 or $20 less per bond than you anticipated.

Column 4. The highest and lowest prices at which bonds traded that day. Unless there is an *f* (for "flat") after the bond listing, buyers are also obliged to pay the seller any accrued but unpaid interest on the bond. The buyer gets the money back, of course, when the company makes its semiannual interest payment.

Column 5. The last price at which bonds were traded. There is generally no way of telling how many bonds traded at this closing price. We have no idea from the listings whether just one Exxon bond or 25 of the 26 bonds traded were sold for 95½. Of course, if the high and low price for the day were the same (as in the case of the Detroit Edison bonds), we can be sure that all the bonds sold at that single price.

Column 6. The change in the closing price from the previous day. For example, the Citicorp bond closed at 91⅛ ($911.25), up ⅛ from the previous close of 91 ($910).

With the exception of convertible issues, price movements in bonds generally reflect changes in interest rates in the economy. If interest rates go up, the prices of existing bonds must go down in order to make them as attractive to investors as newly issued bonds. If interest rates go down, bond prices rise.

The longer the remaining term of the bond, the more it will fluctuate in value. Thus investors tempted by the generally high yields on longer-term bonds must consider that they bear more risk.

U.S. Treasury Bonds and Notes

U.S. Treasury bonds are government debts that mature ten years or more from their date of issue. U.S. Treasury notes mature in more than one year and less than ten from their issue date. Both pay interest twice a year and are backed by the ultimate source of dollar-denominated credit, the U.S. Government. *Uncle Sam won't guarantee that the money will be worth much, but he certainly can guarantee that owners of Treasury bonds and notes will be paid every penny they are owed, on time.*

Treasury bonds and notes are initially sold at auctions. Afterwards they are traded "over the counter" by hundreds of dealers linked together by a computer system. Unlike the over-the-counter market for stocks, this market is very large, very liquid, and very efficient. Billions of dollars' worth of government securities change hands every day, usually in blocks of a million dollars' worth or more. Individual investors can buy or sell in this market through commercial banks and securities brokers. Commissions are relatively low, and for those in a hurry, the proceeds of a sale can be made available in cash the next business day.

Column 1. The annual interest, paid in semiannual checks. Treasury bonds and notes are issued in $1,000 denominations. So the 7 percent security in the first row of the table pays $70 a year in two installments of $35. Note how much the interest rate varies from security to security. That's because some were issued in the late

(TABLE 3)

TREASURY BONDS AND NOTES*

1	2	3
RATE	MATURITY MO/YR	BID
7	Sept96n	99:25
8¾	Oct97n	106:15
13⅜	Aug01	137:31
7⅝	Feb02-07	98:25
8⅛	May21	100:20

*Transaction information for illustration only

1970's and early 1980's paying rates as high as 15 percent.

Column 2. The year in which the bond matures and the government is obligated to pay back the $1,000 face value. This sample list is, of course, quite abbreviated. Over 200 separate issues of bonds and notes are traded each day, with the figures listed in order of the maturity date.

Notice the 7⅝ percent issue, with what appears to be a double maturity date (02-07). That means the bond must be redeemed at face value by Feb.2007, but the govern-

4	5	6
		ASK
ASKED	CHG	YLD
99:27	+3	7.04
106:17	+2	7.30
138:03	..	7.62
98:25	+1	7.75
100:22	+4	8.06

ment has the option of redeeming it any time after Feb. 2002. The government's decision on when to redeem the bond will depend on interest rates in 2002 and beyond. If Uncle Sam can refinance the debt at a lower rate, the bond will probably be called.

An *n* following the month means the security is a note, originally issued to mature in less than ten years. The distinction means little to investors in the secondary Treasury market.

Column 3. The "Bid" is the highest price dealers were willing to pay at the close of the trading day. The number is a percentage of the $1,000 face value. Confusingly, the numbers after the period are not 100ths of a percent, but 32nds. So the bid of 99:25 on the first security means that dealers will pay 99 and 25/32nds of the $1,000 face value of the note, or $997.81. Likewise, the 137:31 bid on the 13⅜ bond of August 2001 is equal to $1,379.70. Practice the arithmetic a little with a pocket calculator; you'll find it isn't as hard as it looks.

Column 4. The "Asked" figure is the lowest price at which dealers were willing to sell the security at the end of the trading day. The difference between the bid and asked price is typically quite small; 4 represents only $1.25. That narrow range is an indication of just how deep and liquid the government bond market is. Occasionally, though, the gap balloons to as much as $10 on less heavily traded issues, proving the government bond market is a good market, but not a perfect one.

Column 5. The "Change" is the difference between the closing bid that day and the closing bid the previous day. Day-to-day movements in bond prices are typically small relative to stocks. Don't be fooled, though; this is hardly a sedate market. For the big traders who buy hundreds of millions' worth of securities daily with borrowed funds, an unanticipated movement of a few 32nds can mean the loss of enormous sums.

Column 6. The "Ask Yield" is the yield to maturity, the annualized profit that an investor would make by buying the security at the asked price and holding it until the government returns the $1,000 principle. Unlike the bid and asked figures, the numbers after the period are 100ths. So 8.06 means what it says:

Note that "yield to maturity" is crucially different from the "current yield" in the listings for corporate bonds. It includes both the annual interest earnings and any gain or loss in capital value between the purchase date and the date of redemption.

Consider, for example, the 13⅜ bond of August 2001. Its current yield for a new purchaser is about 9.6 percent—far more than the 7.62 percent listed in the yield column. But part of the profit from the $133.75 annual interest will go to offset the difference between what an investor would pay for the bond today ($1,389.40) and the $1,000 the government will return in August 2001. It takes a fancy pocket calculator to calculate bond yields. Happily, they are listed in the paper.

U.S. Treasury Strips

Zero-coupon bonds—bonds that pay all their accumulated interest at maturity—are much in demand for a variety of reasons. Big investors like them because their value changes so rapidly in response to changes in interest rates in the economy. And many small investors like them because they know exactly how much money (interest and principal) they will end up with after one or two or twenty years.

So some very clever Wall Street types have created zero-coupon bonds by taking apart standard U.S. Treasury securities and putting them back together in a slightly different form. Here's how it works.

Consider an ordinary 8 percent, 20-year U.S. Treasury bond. It consists of the Treasury's promise to pay $40 every six months (half of the $80 annual interest), plus $1,000 at the end of the twentieth year. If you bought, say, 25 of them, Uncle Sam would owe you $1,000 every six months, plus $25,000 at the end of 20 years. Each of these $1,000 promises-to-pay could thus be "stripped" off the package of 25 bonds and resold to investors as zero-coupon bonds maturing sequentially every six months. Meanwhile, the $25,000 payment due in 20 years could be sold as 25 separate zero-coupon bonds with face values of $1,000 that matured in 20 years.

Once you know how to read the tables for Treasury notes and bonds, interpreting the tables for U.S. Treasury Strips is a snap.

(TABLE 4)

U.S. TREASURY STRIPS*

1	2	3		4	5
MAT	TYPE	BID	ASKED	CHG	ASK YLD.
Nov 97	ci	66:05	66:09	+1	7.43
May 99	np	58:03	58:07	+1	7.72
Nov 21	bp	9:15	9:18	+2	8.08

*Transaction information for illustration only

Column 1. The month and the year in which the Treasury will pay the bond owner the $1,000 face value. Note that, unlike ordinary Treasury bonds, there is no face-value interest rate. The interest on a zero-coupon bond is implicit—the difference between what you pay for the bond and what you receive at maturity.

Column 2. The symbol "ci" stands for coupon interest, meaning the strip security has been assembled from the coupon interest due on many ordinary Treasury bonds. "Np" stands for principle from a Treasury note; "bp" stands for principle from a Treasury bond. As a practical matter, it doesn't matter where the value of a strip is derived: No matter how you slice it, the strip is a U.S. Government guarantee to pay $1,000 at the maturity date.

Column 3. The Bid and Asked figures are identical to the figures in ordinary Treasury bond tables. The number 66:05 means 66⅟₃₂ percent of $1,000, or $661.56.

Column 4. The change from the previous day at the close of trading is in 32nds. So +1 means an increase ⅟₃₂ of $10, or 31 cents.

Column 5. The yield is the interest to maturity (in ordinary percentage notation) received by an investor who pays the asking price for the strip. Thus an investor who paid 58:07 ($582.19) today for Uncle Sam's promise to pay 100:00 ($1,000) in May 1999 would be receiving the equivalent of 7.72 percent interest.

Government Agency Bonds

Dealers in U.S. Treasury securities also buy and sell securities issued by two dozen other U.S. government agencies, non-profit corporations chartered by Congress, and international development agencies supported by governments. Some newspapers only list the more popular agency securities daily and provide a more comprehensive listing on Sundays.

The tables are usually grouped after Treasury bonds and notes. Notations for all bonds are identical: we illustrate them with listings from the Federal Home Loan Bank. Most agency bonds are relatively safe because they are backed by substantial assets. *Keep in mind, though, that not all bonds with the word "federal" in their names are guaranteed by the U.S. Treasury. Nor are all such securities exempt from state and local taxes.* Remember, too, that while agency bonds pay higher interest rates than Treasury issues, the market is considerably thinner. Should you need to sell some in a hurry, you may get back less than you expected.

(TABLE 5)

AGENCY BONDS*

FEDERAL HOME LOAN BANK

1	2	3	4	5
RATE	MAT.	BID	ASKED	YLD.
6.90	2-97	99:04	99:14	7.18
9.25	11-98	108:17	108:15	7.25
8.60	1-00	105:17	105:25	7.60

*Transaction information for illustration only.

Column 1. The annual interest rate on the security. With few exceptions, interest is paid in two semiannual installments.

Column 2. The month and year the security matures. With very few exceptions, agency securities contain no "call" provision. That means the issuing agency does not have the right to redeem the bond for the original issue price before the maturity date.

Column 3. The price dealers were willing to pay at the close of the trading day. Prices are quoted like Treasury bonds and notes. The number before the period is a percentage, while the number after is 32nds of a percent. With Agency bonds selling in units of $1,000, it is easy to translate the percentage into a dollar figure. A bid of, say, 99:04 on a security selling for $1,000 is equal to 99 and ⁴⁄₃₂nds of $1,000, or $991.25.

But while some agency bonds are issued in $1,000 multiples, others come in multiples of $5,000, $10,000, $25,000, or even $100,000. Here is an abbreviated list:

AGENCY	MINIMUM	GOVT. GUARANTEED?
Asian Development Bank	$ 1,000	no
Export-Import Bank	$ 5,000	yes
Federal Farm Credit	$ 1,000	no
Federal Home Loan Bank	$10,000	no
Federal National Mortgage Assn	$10,000	no
Govt National Mortgage Assn	$ 5,000	yes
World Bank	$ 1,000	no

Column 4. The price at which dealers were willing to sell, again quoted as a percentage of issue price. Should

you buy an agency bond, you'll also have to figure in any accrued but unpaid interest since the last semiannual installment.

Column 5. The yield to maturity. That's the annualized return you would get if you bought the security for the asked price and held it to maturity. For securities selling below 100, this return consists of the semiannual interest, plus the gain when the agency redeems the bond for face value. For securities selling above 100, the profit is the interest, less the capital loss when the security is redeemed.

Treasury Bills

Treasury bills (T-bills) are government securities that mature in one year or less. T-bills are initially sold in maturities of 91 days, three months, six months, nine months, and one year and in minimum denominations of $10,000. You can buy newly issued T-bills direct from the Federal Reserve. Or you can buy them in the secondary, "over-the-counter" government securities market. Commercial banks and securities brokers are happy to do the paper work for a small commission.

Reading the newspaper tables requires a little understanding of how T-bills differ from longer-term government bonds and notes. Bonds and notes pay interest twice a year. T-bills, by contrast, pay interest only indirectly through the device of the "discount." The buyer initially pays less than the $10,000 face amount of the bill— perhaps, $9,700. When the bill expires, the government returns the $10,000 face amount. The $300 difference, or discount, is the interest earned by the investor.

(TABLE 6)

TREASURY BILLS*

1	2	3	4
MAT. DATE	BID	ASKED	YIELD
	DISCOUNT		
1993			
4-18	7.38	7.32	7.43
4-25	7.44	7.38	7.50
5-2	7.57	7.51	7.65
1994			
1-23	8.57	8.51	9.10
2-20	8.65	8.61	9.26

*Transaction information for illustration only.

Column 1. The month and day on which the bill matures and the investor's money is returned. Very-short-term bills are available on a weekly maturity basis. Longer maturities have somewhat longer intervals between maturities.

Column 2. It looks like an interest rate, printed out to two decimal places. But it's really a backhanded way of stating the price that dealers were willing to pay for the security at the close of the trading day.

Here's how to think about it: Dealers figure how much they are willing to pay for a bill in dollars and cents. Then they divide the discount (the difference between what the dealer is willing to pay and the $10,000 face value) by the face value and figure the annualized yield to maturity.

Confused? Try it with numbers: A dealer says he will pay $9,700 for a bill that will mature to its $10,000 face value in four months. He then divides the discount of $300 ($10,000 minus $9,700) by the $10,000 face value. $300 divided by $10,000 equals 3 percent for one-third of a year. On an annualized basis, the interest is three times that much, or 9 percent. So a dealer who bids "9.00" for a bill due to mature in four months is really offering to pay $9,700 for the bill.

Column 3. This "asked" figure works like the bid. It is a weird way of stating the price at which dealers are willing to sell the security at the close of the trading day. Another example might help:

Say a dealer is willing to sell a bill due to mature in four months for $9,702. The discount is $298 ($10,000 minus $9,702). Dividing the $298 discount by the $10,000 face value, we get 2.98 percent. On an annualized basis, that equals 3 times 2.98, or 8.94 percent. So a dealer who asks "8.94" for a bill due to mature in four months is really offering to sell the bill for $9,702.

Two additional thoughts: No. 1, *the "asked" number*

is always smaller than the "bid." That may not look right, but it is. The more you pay for a Treasury bill, the lower the interest return will be. No. 2, the diference between the bid and the asked price for Treasury bills is sometimes only pennies. Dealers can still make big money, though, because they trade tens of thousands of bills every day.

Column 4. The yield is the actual annualized yield that an investor would receive if he or she paid the price the dealers are asking and then held the bill to maturity. For investors, it's the one that really counts.

When bid and asked figures are calculated, the discount is divided by the $10,000 face. That was very convenient for the clerks who had to do the arithmetic quickly before the invention of electronic calculators. But the resulting number always under-estimates the true return, because the investor never has to plunk down the full $10,000.

For example, if the asking figure on a one-year T-bill is "8.00," the dealers are offering to sell the T-bill for $800 less than $10,000, or $9,200. The investor's yield on the $9,200 is $800 divided by $9,200, or 8.70 percent.

Still confused? Ignore everything reported in the tables except the yield. That allows you to compare the return on T-bills with the return on other investments.

Tax-Exempt Bonds

Tax-exempt bonds are the borrowings of state and local governments, as well as public agencies that invest in housing, irrigation, electric power generation, toll roads, industrial development, and practically anything else that has some public purpose. As the name implies, the interest income (but not any realized capital gains) from these bonds is free from federal tax. Most states also exempt from taxes the interest income on bonds issued within their borders.

Tax-exempts are divided into two broad categories: "general obligation" bonds, backed by the taxing power of a government, and "revenue" bonds, backed by a specific stream of income generated by a project or group of projects. In recent years, the majority of new issues are in the revenue category. And with a few exceptions, the bonds listed in daily newspapers are revenue bonds.

Column 1. The name of the issuing authority of government. Literally thousands of different entities have tax-exempt bonds outstanding. But only about 75 of the largest and most active issues are listed in the papers on a daily basis. The information can still be quite useful, though, even if you don't own or aren't planning to buy one of the listed issues; other bonds are likely to track the general price trends.

Note the two Valdez listings. These are bonds issued to finance antipollution equipment at the Alaskan oil tanker port of Valdez. But the interest payments are guaranteed by private oil companies rather than the city of Valdez. Such arrangements are increasingly common. The only way to find out who is backing a bond is to read the

(TABLE 7)

TAX-EXEMPT BONDS*

1	2
AGENCY	COUPON
Bat Park City Auth NY	6⅜s
Intermountain Pwr	10½s
MAC	8s
Valdez (Exxon)	5½s
Valdez (Sohio)	6s

*Transaction information for illustration only.

HOW TO READ THE FINANCIAL PAGES

original prospectus. Any bond dealer who really wants your business should be able to get you one.

Column 2. The annual percentage interest provided by the bond issuer. This payment—actually two semiannual payments—is called the "coupon" because older bonds have interest coupons attached to them. To collect the interest on such "bearer" bonds, you must clip off the coupon on the specified date and present it to a bank acting as agent for the borrower. Or, you can leave bearer bonds on deposit with a broker, who clips and cashes the coupons and deposits the money in your brokerage account.

3	4	5	6
MAT.	BID	ASKED	CHG.
14	68	72	−½
18	100	104	. .
91	99½	103½	. .
07	64½	66½	+ ½
07	66	68	. .

Since 1983 the federal government has required all new bonds to be issued in "registered" form. With registered bonds, there are no coupons to clip. Interest payments are automatically mailed to the registered owner of the bonds. *The only real disadvantage to owners is that registration creates a "paper trail."* Paper who don't want the government to know how much money they have don't like that. . . .

Column 3. The last two digits of the year in which the bonds mature. Tax-exempt bonds are typically issued in serial form. For example, an agency may borrow $100 million, with $5 million maturing in each of the next 20 years. That may be convenient for issuing agencies that want to pay off the debts as the project itself wears out. But it fragments the tax-exempt bond market into more, smaller issues of bonds.

Longer-term bonds usually pay higher yields. But owners also incur more risk because fluctuations in interest rates in the economy will have a greater impact on the market value of the bond. Remember, too, that some tax-exempt bonds contain call provisions. These give the borrower the option of paying off the bonds prematurely, should interest rates fall.

Column 4. The price, quoted as a percentage of face value, that dealers are willing to pay for the bond. Most tax-exempts with maturities exceeding a year are issued in $5,000 denominations. So the Valdez (Exxon) bond has a bid of 64½ percent of $5,000, or $3,225.

Buyers of tax-exempts are obliged to pay the interest accrued between semiannual payment dates. These Valdez (Exxon) 5½-percent bonds are scheduled to pay $137.50 every six months (that's half of 5½ percent, times $5,000). So if a dealer purchased one of these bonds three months after a payment date, he would owe an extra $68.75 in accrued interest to the seller.

Column 5. The price, again quoted as a percentage of face value, that dealers are willing to sell the bond. The asked price on the Valdez (Exxon) issue is 66½, which translates as 66½ percent of $5,000, or $3,325, plus accrued interest.

The difference between the bid and asked price in this case was two percentage points. That is relatively low compared with the four percentage point spread for most listed issues and very low compared with the six or eight percentage point spread that is common for less-actively traded bonds. But it is quite high in comparison with stocks traded on an exchange. The lesson here is that buying and selling tax-exempt bonds is very expensive. *Buy tax-exempts only for the long haul.* It rarely pays to buy them with the expectation of selling them a few months or years later.

Column 6. The change in the bid price since the previous day.

Mutual Fund Quotations

Mutual funds are companies that sell shares to the public, then invest the proceeds in stocks, bonds, and other securities. Some are quite specialized, investing in only one industry (gold mining) or one country (Korea). Others diversify their holdings across many industries and many countries.

Compare an "open-end" mutual fund with an ordinary corporation. Ordinary corporations issue new shares infrequently. If you want to own some, you typically buy them from someone who already owns a piece of the company. An "open-end" mutual fund, by contrast, has no fixed number of outstanding shares. The fund grows when investors buy shares directly from the fund or its sales agents. When investors wish to sell the shares, they sell them back to the fund under terms set in the original sales contract.

Funds are set up by investment companies that profit

by taking a percentage of the assets of the fund as fees each year. In order to avoid paying corporate income taxes, mutual funds must pay out all their earnings to share owners. *Most funds allow investors to reinvest their earnings automatically. But reinvested or not, share owners are liable for personal income taxes on earnings in the year they are declared by the mutual fund.*

(TABLE 8)

MUTUAL FUNDS*

1	2	3
	LAST	CHG.
Dean Witter:		
AmVal t	19.56	−.50
Premier p	9.79	+.06
Sears TE np	11.69	+.05
Fidelity Invest:		
EmgGro r	15.22	−.57
Value fn	31.67	−.52

*Transaction information for illustration only

Column 1. The name of the mutual fund. Several hundred open-end funds can be found in the weekly listings. Where an investment company (like Fidelity Investment) sponsors several funds, they are grouped alphabetically under the sponsor's name.

The letter "n" after a fund means that it does not charge an initial "load" or sales fee to buy shares. The letter "r" means that you do pay a fee to sell the shares back to the mutual fund—typically a few percent of the share value. A "p" means that an annual charge is levied against shareholders to cover the cost of selling more shares. This is sometimes referred to as a 12(b)1 Plan, after the Securities and Exchange Commission rule that made these charges legal. A letter "t" means that both a redemption fee and a 12(b)1 Plan fee are charged.

Last and least: An "f" means that the asset value quoted is not quite up to date—it probably is the previous day's figure.

Column 2. Each share in a mutual fund represents a tiny fraction of the whole portfolio—often dozens of different securities. The figure is the market value of one share's worth of the underlying securities at the close of the previous trading day. For example, behind every share of Dean Witter's Premier Fund is $9.79 worth of assets. If you owned a share and chose to sell it back to the fund, you would receive $9.79.

In the case of Fidelity's Emerging Growth Fund, however, you would get a bit less than $15.22 because Fidelity apparently charges a small redemption fee. Note that funds will generally also sell you shares at the asset value, plus any posted sales fee.

Column 3. The change in the net asset value of a share from the previous week.

Money Market Mutual Funds

Money market funds are mutual funds that invest in very safe, very liquid short-term securities, such as U.S. Treasury bills, bank certificates of deposit, and secured loans to large corporations. Investors' income consists of the interest earned, less charges by the sponsoring investment firm. Some money market funds are available only to specific groups—for example, customers of a securities broker or members of non-profit groups such as the American Association of Retired Persons. Others cater only to the wealthy, requiring a minimum initial investment as high as $20,000. But most are delighted to do business with people willing to invest a minimum of $1,000 to $2,500.

Money market funds are, for most practical purposes, interchangeable with money market accounts at banks. Like banks, funds try to discourage heavy use of the checking privilege; most funds manage this by placing a $250 or $500 minimum on the size of checks that can be written. But unlike bank accounts, money market funds are not insured by the federal government. They are still very safe, however, because shares in a money market fund are specific ownership claims on very secure assets.

Column 1. The name of the fund. Roughly two hundred are listed weekly in major newspapers.

The letter *f* indicates that the figures are from the day previous to the standard reporting day. The letter *c:* the fund invests primarily in municipal bonds, so the return to investors is largely exempt from federal tax. The letter *b:* the yield shown is the yield earned by the average size account. Smaller accounts earned less, larger accounts more. This usually arises because the fund charges a fixed monthly minimum—say $3—to maintain the account. If an account is very small, the minimum may eat up a good portion of the earnings.

Slightly different methods are used to calculate the current interest return on funds. The letter *a* indicates that a fund includes capital gains and losses in the computation of yield, as well as actual interest payments on the securities in its portfolio. This can be important; if interest rates in the economy go up or down rapidly, the fund will incur capital losses or gains, and the reported yield will be distorted by as much as a full percentage point for a brief period. *Moral: If you happen to be attracted to a fund that includes capital changes in its reported yields, be sure to compare its record over several weeks before investing.*

Column 2. The number of days until the average security in the fund's portfolio matures. The longer the average maturity, the greater the risk that the income earned by the fund will include capital losses or gains. That's why no money market fund allows its portfolio maturity to become very long; three months is exceptional. So the risk of losing more than a fraction of a percent of assets is very small, even for the funds with the longest average maturity.

Column 3. The average yield, at the annual rate, currently earned by investors after all expenses charged by management. When comparing these rates with the rates on longer-term savings such as bank certificates, remember to make allowances for compounding. A money market fund credits interest to your account every day. So you earn interest on your interest on a daily basis. That can matter; 8 percent compounded daily is the equivalent of 8.33 percent annually.

Money market funds investing in the same types of securities pay roughly equivalent rates of return. Why, then, do the average yields in the listings vary from 5.21 to 8.36 percent?

The two funds paying less than six percent invest in securities exempt from federal tax. They represent good value for investors in high tax brackets, whose after-tax return on a taxable fund paying seven or eight percent would be lower. For example, a tax-free 5.21 percent is the equivalent of a taxable 7.24 percent for an investor in the 28-percent tax bracket.

That explains the biggest differences in yields, but there are other considerations, too. Some funds pay about a half percentage point below the highest yielding funds because they have a policy of investing only in government securities.

Investing in government funds may make sense for two reasons. They are a bit safer than other funds because their investments are backed by the U.S. Treasury. *Perhaps more important, the interest on government funds is exempt from state and local income taxes*. This can matter quite a bit in high tax states such as New York, California, and Wisconsin. Still other funds invest in securities that are insured by big life insurance companies. They are very safe. How much safer than uninsured funds (or how much less safe than government-backed funds) is not clear.

Closed-End Bond Funds and Publicly Traded Mutual Funds

Most mutual funds are "open-ended": You buy shares from the sponsoring investment company that invests the proceeds in common stocks, bonds, precious metals, etc. Should you want to sell the shares, the investment company buys them back for the underlying value of the assets the shares represent, less any redemption fees.

But there is another, lesser known type of mutual fund which is "closed-ended." These funds sell a fixed number of shares to the public. After the initial public offering, those who want to invest must buy shares from the other owners, much the way investors buy shares of IBM or General Motors. By the same token, the only way to sell shares in a closed-end fund is to find someone who wants to buy them.

Closed-end funds are listed in two separate newspaper columns: "Closed-End Funds," consisting of funds that invest primarily in bonds, and "Publicly Traded Funds," which invest in common stocks and securities convertible into common stock.

Buying and selling shares in either category is easy, for there are established markets for fund shares. Some are listed on the New York and American stock exchanges. Others are sold "over the counter" by brokers linked by computer. The heavily traded closed-end funds are listed in daily newspapers along with ordinary corporate stocks. A more complete listing, with extra information, is printed weekly.

Column 1. The name of the fund. Information on about thirty funds is available on a weekly basis. Some of these funds are diversified common stock funds that buy stocks for growth potential and dividends. Most follow some specialized investment strategy. For example, the Korea Fund invests only in Korean stocks.

Column 2. The net value, per share, of the underlying assets. For example, a ten-million-share fund with assets that could be sold for $50 million would have a net asset value per share of $5.00.

The letter *a* means ex-dividend. Today's purchasers of the shares would not receive a recently declared dividend. The letter *b* means the net asset value is reported as of the previous Thursday rather than Friday.

Column 3. Where shares are traded on an exchange, the price is the Friday closing price. Where shares are

(TABLE 10)

PUBLICLY TRADED MUTUAL FUNDS*

1	2	3	4
		STOCK	%
FUND	NAV	PRICE	DIFF
Adm Exp	17.85	16¼	−9
BakerFen	a40.88	35	−14.4
Korea	11.31	13	+ 14.9
Mexico	31.04	29	−6.4

*Transaction information for illustration only.

traded over the counter, the figure is the price at which dealers who own the stock are willing to sell it to other dealers. If you buy listed shares from a broker, expect to pay a regular brokerage commission. Shares sold over the counter are usually marked up by a few percent from the dealer-to-dealer asking price.

Column 4. The percentage difference between the share price and the net asset value.

Note that three out of four of the funds in our sample are selling for less than their NAV. In other words, if the managers of these funds sold off the assets and delivered the cash to the fund owners, the owners would be better off. Why don't they, then? Fund managers say that, given time, the market will recognize its error and the gap will close. Cynics say the fund managers put their own interests above those of the shareholders. If a fund's assets were liquidated, after all, there would be no more salaries and no more salmon and white wine lunches at fund expense.

Funds trading below net asset value are often an interesting speculation, in part, because they deliver more bang for a buck: why buy $10,000 worth of bonds for $10,000 when you can have them for $9,000? In part, because some large investor may come along, take control of the fund from the managers, and liquidate the assets.

Some funds trade above their net asset value. That's because the public values the expertise of the managers, or simply has no other convenient way to make the investment. Few investors, for example, would have any idea of how to choose Korean stocks for their own portfolios and are thus willing to pay for the right to buy into the portfolio someone else assembled.

Stock Options

Stock options are the right to buy or sell shares of common stock for some agreed-upon price and time period. For example, I might sell you the option to purchase 100 shares of IBM stock for $150 a share any time in the next three months. Options trading on organized markets is anonymous. Brokers match buyers and sellers, just as they do on stock exchanges. Once the options agreement is made, however, it becomes a contract between the exchange and the investors. *Thus the purchaser of an option never need worry whether or not the seller will be willing or able to honor his commitment.*

The reasons for trading options varies. Conservative investors use options to reduce risk and raise their expected return by selling an option to buy stock they already own. Other investors buy options as an alternative to buying the underlying stock. That generally gives an investor more bang for the buck—bigger profits when the stock rises and, alas, bigger losses when the stock falls. Still others use option strategies as an alternative to selling "short" the underlying stock. They win if the stock falls in value.

As this is being written, options on over 200 stocks were available on the American, New York, Pacific, and Philadelphia exchanges as well as the Chicago Board of Trade. Options trading in the 100 most active stocks sold

(TABLE 11)

STOCK OPTIONS*

1	2	3	
OPTION & NY CLOSE	STRIKE PRICE	CALLS-LAST	
		APR	JUL
IBM	90	r	r
107	95	11¾	14
107	100	7¼	11
107	105	2¾	8½
107	110	⅝	5¾
107	115	⅙	3⅜
107	120	r	2¼
107	125	r	⅞

*Transaction information for illustration only.

over the counter is set to begin soon. Listings for all the markets, including the proposed options for over-the-counter stocks, are identical.

Column 1. IBM is, of course, the big computer company whose stock is listed on the New York Stock Exchange. Options are available on most heavily traded stocks, and in particular, on stocks whose prices are volatile. Some stocks, by the way, are listed on two

---

4

		PUTS-LAST	
OCT	APR	JUL	OCT
s	1/16	7/8	s
16½	⅛	1¾	3
14¼	¼	3	4⅜
11½	1	4¾	6
9	4¼	7	8⅝
r	8¾	10½	r
4¾	13½	r	r
r	r	r	

exchanges. The "NY Close" is the closing price of the stock itself on the exchange in New York.

Column 2. The "Strike Price" is the price at which the owner of the option has the right to buy or sell the underlying stock.

Notice that IBM options are traded at eight different strike prices. The range, from $90 a share to $125, reflects an estimate made by exchange officials of where IBM stock might end up in coming months. With the stock trading for $107 today, the exchange apparently doesn't believe that anyone will want to bet that the price will fall very far below $90 or very much above $125.

The exchanges aim to please: where the underlying stock trades for less than $25, strike prices are set in increments of $2.50 rather than $5. New strike prices are added as the stock price approaches the high or low end of the range.

Column 3. A "Call" option is the right to buy shares of stock at the strike price anytime until the third Friday of the specified month. Thus a "July 105" call on IBM is the right to buy IBM stock for $105 a share anytime between now and the third Friday in July. The price of this option, known as the "premium," is $8.50 a share. Since calls are bought and sold for 100 share units, it would cost you $850 (plus brokerage commissions) to buy a July 105 call.

Alternatively, you could sell a July 105 call for $850, less broker commissions. Selling the call, in theory, obliges you to deliver 100 shares of the stock for $105 a share. But the buyer of the call option usually wants the profit, not the stock. And the seller of the call option doesn't want to go to the expense of purchasing the stock for delivery to the option owner. *So when options are exercised, the option seller is permitted to settle his account by paying the difference between the current price of the stock and the strike price.* If, in July, IBM were selling for $111, the option seller would pay out the $6 (times 100) difference between the $105 strike price and the $111 market price of the stock.

Call options in IBM are sold for three different dates and eight different strike prices. Options at strike prices below the current price of the stock are known as "in the money" options. Note that longer call options at the same strike price cost more. That stands to reason: the longer the option runs, the greater the chance the stock price will rise and the speculation will be profitable.

A letter *r* in the premium column means the option wasn't traded that day. A letter *s* means that no option was offered.

Column 4. A "Put" is the right to sell the stock for the strike price. So an October 110 put is the right to sell IBM stock for $110 a share anytime between now and the third Friday in October.

A put is a bet against a stock. If the price of the stock is more than the strike price when the put option expires, the option is worthless. On the other hand, if IBM stock were to fall to, say, $90 a share in October, the October

110 put would be worth at least $20 a share, or $2,000 for the 100-share option.

Two general points to remember about options on stocks. *First, brokerage commissions can be a very high percentage of the premium.* You might end up paying 10 or 20 percent of the value of the option to buy or sell. *Second, the market in most options is very thin.* And with few buyers or sellers in the game, premiums can be volatile.

Long Term Options

Ordinary stock options allow you to bet on the price of a stock a few months into the future. But what if you want to bet on the price in two years?

(TABLE 12)

LONG TERM OPTIONS*

OPTION/EXPIRATION/STRIKE	LAST
AT&T Jan 95 25	15⅜
AT&T Jan 95 35	6
AT&T Jan 95 35p	1½
AT&T Jan 96 40	3

*Transaction information for illustration only

Where investors have a will, Wall Street has a way. The exchanges now make markets for long term options for a few dozen stocks.

Note that the long term option table is an abbreviated form of the table for the more common, shorter-term options. The first row shows an AT&T call option at a strike price of 25, which expires in January 1995. At the last trade of the day, an option to purchase AT&T stock at a price of $25 a share anytime until Jan. 1995 sold for 15⅜ ($15.38).

The letter "p" after the strike price indicates a put. Thus the option to sell AT&T shares for 35 anytime until Jan. 1995 sold for $1.50.

Stock Index Options

A stock index option is a bet on the direction and size of a change of a stock index. Most of the indexes used are broad gauges of stock values. But options are also written on specialized indexes, such as the computer technology index, the transportation stock index, and the oil stock index.

Trading in index options is one of the fastest ways to make money on Wall Street. Unfortunately, index option trading is also one of the fastest ways to lose money. This casino-like quality has made index options immensely popular with speculators who want to maximize their bang for each buck. Institutional buyers also find them useful as tools in elaborate hedging and arbitrage strategies. Virtually all the stock and commodities exchanges now trade some form of stock index option. New ones are being created as fast as federal regulators will permit. But the listings all follow the same form.

Column 1. The strike price is the index value at which the owner of the option has the right to buy (in the case of a call) or the right to sell (in the case of a put).

The Standard and Poor 100 index is an index of 100 heavily traded stocks. Note from the data below the table that the index reached a high of 175.54 that day and a low of 173.66 before closing at 173.67. The range of strike prices for which options can be written—here, 160 to 195—reflects the range of levels that traders think the index might plausibly reach in the coming three months. If stock prices soared, the exchange would no doubt agree to trading at still higher strike prices.

Column 2. An investor who buys a call is betting that the index will increase in value before the expiration date, the third Friday of the month listed. The price or "premium" on a call depends on the strike price and the length of time until the expiration date. For example, at the close of trading, one investor was apparently willing to pay another investor $4.50 (4½) for the right to "buy" the index at 175 any time between then and the third Friday in July.

Indexes aren't shares of stock or bushels of wheat. What does it mean to buy or sell one? Nothing is actually bought or sold. When the call expires, the owner of the call simply settles the bet with the seller for the difference between the strike price and the actual index value.

Another example should help make this clearer. Suppose the S&P index stands at 181 when the markets close on the third Friday in July. The owner of a July 175 call is entitled to $6—the difference between 181 and 175. Actually, standard option contracts are written in multiples of 100. Someone who paid 4½ for the July 175 call really paid $450 (4½ × 100). And the value of the July call, if the index is at 181, is 6 times 100, or $600.

What determines the premium on a call? At minimum, a call is always worth the difference between the current level of the option and the strike price. That day, the index closed at 173.67. So the right to buy the index at 165 was worth at least 8.67 (173.67 minus 165). In fact, the June 165 call traded for 11½, almost $3 more than the minimum. Someone was apparently willing to bet that the index would reach 176.5 (165 plus 11½) sometime between then and the third Friday in June. For every option buyer, there must be a seller. So apparently there was also someone willing to bet that the index wouldn't reach 176.5 by June.

Column 3. An investor who buys a put is betting that the index will fall in value by the expiration date.

Consider, for example, the arithmetic behind a June 175 put which sold for $3. Like calls, puts are settled in cash based on the difference between the strike price and the value of the index. So the buyer of the put is betting the index will fall at least as far as 172 (175 minus 3) by the third Friday in June. If the index closed at, say, 164, on the settlement date, the seller would have to pay $1,100 (100 times the difference between 175 and 164).

Option sellers (called option "writers") are under no obligation to wait until the expiration date to find out whether and how much money they owe. They can buy back the options they sold at any time. The act of

(TABLE 12)

INDEX OPTIONS*
S & P 100 INDEX

1		2	
STRIKE		CALLS-LAST	
PRICE	MAY	JUNE	JULY
160	. .	. .	. .
165	9⅜	11½	. .
170	4⅜	6⅛	7½
175	1¼	3	4½
180	3/16	1 3/16	2⅜
185	1/16	⅜	1
190	1/16	1/16	½
195	1/16	1/16	. .

Total call volume 133,984 Total calls open interest 588,759
Total put volume 134,155 Total put open interest 390,053
The index: High 175.54 Low 173.66 Close 173.67, −1.28

*Transaction information for illustration only.

purchasing the option transfers any settlement obligation to the new seller.

The data below the table shows how active the market was in S&P 100 options. That day 134,155 put contracts

	3	
	PUTS-LAST	
MAY	JUNE	JULY
$\frac{1}{16}$	$\frac{1}{16}$	$\frac{3}{16}$
$\frac{1}{16}$	$\frac{3}{16}$	$\frac{7}{16}$
$\frac{5}{16}$	$\frac{7}{8}$	$1\frac{1}{4}$
$2\frac{3}{16}$	3	$3\frac{3}{8}$
$6\frac{3}{8}$	$6\frac{3}{8}$	$6\frac{5}{8}$
$11\frac{3}{8}$	11	$10\frac{1}{8}$
15	..	..
..	..	..

were traded. And at the close of trading there were 390,053 put contracts in existence. Trading in other index options is not nearly so active. The total volume of puts sold that same day on the American Exchange's Computer Technology Index was just 277.

Commodity Futures

A commodity future contract is an agreement between a buyer and seller to trade a specific amount of a commodity at a date in the future: "I agree to sell you A tons of commodity B at $\$C$ a ton for delivery in D months." Got it? Go to the head of the class, or read on.

Organized futures markets for everything from coffee to lumber to platinum have been around for a long time. That's because businesses producing these commodities, along with businesses that use them as raw materials, need futures markets to hedge against the risk of price changes. For example, a jewelry manufacturer that must set catalogue prices a half year in advance might lock in the cost of the gold she uses by purchasing gold in the futures market for delivery in six months. A farmer worried in the spring that corn prices might collapse by harvest time might sell corn for delivery in October.

What works to reduce risk for some also serves to in-

crease risk for others. In fact, many if not most of the buyers and sellers in the futures markets are speculators hoping to profit by correctly predicting changes in commodity prices. For heavily traded commodities, such as corn, wheat, soybeans, and vegetable oils, the average contract is held for only three to five days before it is sold for a gain or loss.

Some speculators are big winners, using the incredible leverage offered by futures contracts to double their investment in weeks. *But take care: by one estimate, five commodity speculators out of six lose money.* And far too many

(TABLE 13)

COMMODITY FUTURES*
CORN (CBT) 5,000 BU.; CENTS PER BU.

1	2		3	4
	OPEN	HIGH	LOW	SETTLE
May	284½	284¾	282½	283¼
July	279¼	279¾	278¾	278¾
Sept	268¾	269½	268	268¾
Dec	263½	264½	262¾	263½
Mar 94	271	272½	271	271¼
May	276	276¾	275½	276¼
July	278	278¼	277¾	278

Est. vol. 20,000; vol. prev. day 16,602;

*Transaction information for illustration only.

commodities brokers are hustlers who don't care whether you end up as one of the five.

By law, commodity futures may only be bought and sold through organized, government-regulated exchanges. The exchange is a go-between, linking like-minded buyers and sellers. But once a contract to deliver this much frozen orange juice concentrate at that many cents per pound is made, the exchange takes the responsibility to enforce the agreement. Technically, commodity future agreements are with the exchange, not the other party. So

| 5 | 6 | | 7 |
| | LIFETIME | | OPEN |
CHANGE	HIGH	LOW	INTEREST
−¾	330	269¾	14,180
..	331	273	51,331
+¼	321½	266½	12,100
+½	295	260¾	5,167
+¾	297	269¼	3,830
+¾	291¼	274½	1,732
+¾	286	276¼	273

open int. 108, 613, −1,408

there is never any worry that it will be necessary to take the other party to court.

Future contracts in corn are traded on the Chicago Board of Trade (CBT) exchange. About fifteen different exchanges offer commodities futures, with virtually no overlap in commodities. The one exchange that does duplicate contracts is the Mid-America Commodity Exchange (MCE). It sponsors trading in "mini-contracts" for corn, soybeans, and what. Mini-contracts are one-fifth the size of regular contracts, the idea is to make commodities trading more accessible to small investors. That can be handy, but be cautious. The volume of trading on the MCE is much smaller than on the senior exchanges, and the contracts may prove to be less liquid.

Immediately following the exchange symbol is the size of the standard contract and the units in which prices are set. Thus corn (and most grains) come in standard units of 5,000 bushels, and prices are quoted in cents per bushel.

Column 1. The month in which the seller agrees to deliver the commodity. Commodity contracts are written for regular intervals specified by the exchange, with the longest contracts stretching about a year into the future.

Investors are betting on price changes. Sellers typically have no wish to deliver the commodity in question, nor do buyers really want to accept delivery. Thus most contracts are liquidated long before the delivery month by a transaction that balances out the original commitment. For example, the seller of eight December contracts for corn (40,000 bushels worth) would simply buy eight December contracts when she wished to stop betting the price of corn would fall.

Past a certain "notice date"—in the case of corn, the last day of the month preceding the delivery month—sellers have the option of meeting their contractual obligation by delivering the commodity. When that happens, some unfortunate buyer designated under the rules of the exchange—usually the person who has held a buying contract longest—has no choice but to accept delivery. The moral: Buyers of corn (or other commodity) futures who don't want to risk finding a trainload of food on the doorstep some fine morning should be sure to liquidate their positions before the notice date.

Column 2. The price at which the first contract of the day was struck. September corn sold for $2.6875 (268¾) per bushel. Corn for delivery in May 1994 went for $2.76.

These prices are really guesses about the future price of corn. Investors on the "buy" side of the contract hope that prices will rise because they have locked in the maximum they will have to pay. Investors on the "sell" side hope prices will fall.

Note one factor, though, that governs the relationship between prices for different monthly contracts. A futures price can never be higher than the price of buying the commodity today, plus lost interest on the investment in the commodity, plus storage and delivery costs. Otherwise, savvy traders could guarantee themselves an automatic profit by purchasing the commodity for cash and selling a futures contract for a like amount.

Column 3. The high and low contract prices for the day. The high for December corn was $2.645 a bushel; the low was $2.6275.

The exchanges impose limits on both the amount a futures price can vary from the closing price on the previous day (in the case of corn, 10 cents a bushel), and the range between the high and low on any single day (for corn, 20 cents a bushel). The idea is to prevent panic trading on news of an important event—for example, freezing weather for the citrus crop. When a limit is reached, the exchange doesn't close. It simply stops trading until a buyer and seller can be found who want to make a deal within the limit range.

Column 4. The price at which the last contract of the day was written. May 1993 corn futures closed at $2.8325; July 1994 closed at $2.78.

Buyers of futures contracts profit when futures prices rise. Suppose, for example, the price of the May 1993 contract rises by 20 cents to $3.0325. A buyer may cash in by selling a May 1993 contract, liquidating his position and realizing a profit of 20 cents a bushel, or $1,000.

The same arithmetic works in reverse for sellers. A seller would be free to close out his position by purchasing a May 1993 contract at a loss of 20 cents a bushel, or $1,000. Both buyers and sellers pay commissions to brokers for each trade. So the buyer who closed out his position would profit by a bit less than $1,000 and the seller would lose a bit more than $1,000.

Column 5. The change in the closing price since the previous trading day. The prices of corn futures fluctuate in units of a quarter of a penny a bushel. This minimum fluctuation (or "tick," in the jargon of the exchanges) varies from commodity to commodity.

The buyer of a May 1993 contract that day was committed to purchase 5,000 bushels of corn for $14,162.50 (5,000 times $2.8325.) Everyone knows the buyer is very unlikely to hold the contract to delivery. But the exchange does want to make certain that the buyer can, if necessary, make good on his commitment. Thus it requires both buyers and sellers to put up five to ten percent of the value of the commodity as margin when the contract is made, much the way a building contractor is sometimes required to put up cash as a performance bond before beginning a project.

At the close of each trading day, the exchange "marks all positions to market." Suppose, for example, the price of May 1993 futures rises 5 cents. At the end of the day, the exchange will credit the margin accounts of everyone on the buy side of the contracts with a nickel a bushel, or $250 in cash per contract. And simultaneously, it will take $250 in cash from the margin accounts of all May 1993 sellers.

Those who receive cash are free to withdraw it from their accounts. When a buyer's or seller's margin is depleted to specified levels, the exchange can demand an infusion of cash. If the investor is unable to meet this call for margin money, his position is automatically liquidated.

Column 6. The range of contract prices since contracts with this delivery date were first created. For July 1993 corn futures, the range was from a high of $3.31 a bushel to a low of $2.73.

Consider how much money might have been made or lost by investors since the contract was created the previous year. Say a seller put down 10 percent as margin just when the contract peaked at $3.31 a bushel. That amounted to an investment of about 33 cents a bushel. By the time the July contract had bottomed out at $2.73, our lucky investor's margin account would have been credited with a profit of 58 cents a bushel (331 minus 273), or almost double his money.

By the same token, of course, a buyer of a July contract at 3.31 would have lost 58 cents a bushel. If he had not been willing or able to replenish his margin account with cash, he would long ago have been closed out.

Column 7. The number of contracts outstanding at the close of the trading day. Note that the open interest in July 1993 contracts is three times as large as the number of May 1993 contracts. That's because investors have been closing out their May positions as the possibility of delivery approaches. Note, too, how few contracts have been written for delivery dates in 1994. That's because businesses that use the futures markets for hedging and hold much of the open interest rarely plan so far ahead.

Some 20,000 contracts (for 100 million bushels of corn) were written that day, reflecting the immense liquidity of the markets for grain futures. By contrast, the futures market for unleaded gasoline had a volume of only 262 contracts. Overall, open interest in corn fell by 1,408 contracts.

Financial Futures

Financial futures are contracts to deliver a financial instrument as a specified time for a specified price. The markets for financial futures work much like the markets for futures in commodities. Only instead of creating contracts for the future delivery of cotton or gold or heating oil, the contracts cover the delivery of U.S. Treasury bonds or German marks or U.S. Treasury bills. So most of the information provided in the key to the commodity futures table also applies to financial futures.

Treasury bond futures are traded on the Chicago Board of Trade (CBT) and the MidAmerica Commodity Exchange. The standard contract is for $100,000 on the CBT and $50,000 on the MCE. Unlike commodity contracts, some variation in what actually has to be delivered is permitted. For example, under exchange rules, Treasury bonds can be any issue of U.S. Treasury bonds with a remaining term of fifteen or more years. Thus a seller could deliver any of twenty issues with different maturity dates. Before trading in financial futures, be sure to find out what the rules of the exchange are.

(TABLE 14)

FINANCIAL FUTURES*
TREASURY BONDS (CBT) — $100,000;
PTS. 32NDS OF 100 PERCENT.

1	2	3	4	5
	OPEN	HIGH	LOW	SETTLE
June	72-05	72-19	71-31	72-01
Sept	71-03	71-18	70-29	70-31
Dec	70-06	70-18	69-31	70-01
Mr94	69-11	69-23	69-04	69-06
June	68-21	68-29	68-13	68-14
Sept	67-31	68-09	67-24	67-24
Dec	67-13	67-20	67-05	67-05
Mr95	66-20	66-20	66-19	66-19
Sept	66-02	66-09	65-20	65-20

Est vol 160,000; vol prev 71,064; open int. 223,423, +1,

*Transaction information for illustration only.

Prices are quoted in fractional 32nds of a percentage point of face value. That is not the case for financial futures on securities with shorter maturities. Financial futures in Treasury bills and insured bank deposits trade in 100ths of a percentage point of face value.

6	7	8	9
CHG	YIELD SETTLE	CHG.	OPEN INTEREST
+2	11.632	−.010	146,197
+2	11.814	−.011	42,399
+2	11.978	−.011	11,116
+2	12.129	−.011	8,488
+1	12.266	−.006	6,194
..	12.394	..	3,818
..	12.506	..	1,684
−1	12.613	+.006	976
−2	12.802	+.012	1,374

Column 1. The month in which delivery of the bonds is due. Less than 3 percent of financial futures contracts are actually settled by delivery. *As with commodity futures, most traders close out their positions by undertaking the opposite transaction.* For example, an investor who is obliged to sell a bond in December 1994 can end the obligation by contracting to buy a bond in December 1994.

Column 2. The price at which the first contract of the day was struck. June 1993 contracts opened at 72-05, which translates as 72 and 5/32nds of a percent (72.1563 percent) of the $100,000 face value. To put it another way, someone contracted to buy a Treasury bond with a $100,000 value at maturity for delivery in June 1993 at a price of $72,156.30.

Column 3. The highest price at which contracts were written. For example, the June 1993s peaked at 72-19, which is 72 and 19/32nds of a percent of face value, or $72,593.80.

Column 4. The lowest price at which contracts were written. Again looking at the June 1993s, the figure is 71-31, or 71 and 31/32nds of a percent of face value, or $71,968.70. The difference between the high and low that day was 20/32nds of a percentage point. Under exchange rules, by the way, the limit on the trading range for a single day is 64/32nds.

Column 5. The last price at which contracts were written that trading day.

Column 6. The change in the closing price since the previous day, in 32nds of a percentage point. Our June 1993s were up 2, which is 2/32nds of a percentage point of $100,000, or $62.50. That is a very modest change in price. But remember, one of the attractions of the futures market is that investors need not put much down to play the game. In the case of Treasury bonds, just $1,500 is required as margin. So an increase in value of $62.50 represented an increase of over 4 percent in a single day, or an annualized rate of gain of 1,520 percent!

Column 7. Futures for Treasury bonds and other fixed-return securities are often referred to as interest rate futures, and for good reason. Bond prices change in response to changes in interest rates. If interest rates rise, bond prices fall. And, of course, if interest rates fall, bond prices rise. *So an investment in a Treasury bond future is really a bet about the course of interest rates between the day you write the contract and the delivery date.*

The yield column is the interest return that corresponds to the closing price for the bond future. For the June 1993s that yield was 11.632 percent. Put it another way: if an investor purchased a Treasury bond in June 1993 for 72-01 ($72,031.25) and held the bond fifteen years to maturity, the annualized return would be 11.632 percent.

Column 8. The change in yield since the close of trading the previous day. For the June bonds, an increase in bond value of 2/32nds of a percentage point is equivalent to a reduction in yield of .01 percent.

Column 9. Open interest is the number of standard contracts in existence. There are 146,197 contracts outstanding for the June 1993 bonds. Open interest for other delivery dates is considerably less, but a quick look at the numbers show that this has become an incredibly large market. At the $1,600 initial margin requirement for buyer and seller, the 146,197 figure represents a total cash investment of $438.591 million (3,000 times 146,197).

The estimated volume of trading in all Treasury bond contracts was 160,000. Put it another way: investors in this market traded commitments with a total value of $16 billion!

Foreign Exchange

Currencies are traded electronically through a global "over-the-counter" market linking large banks and government agencies. This market is enormous and growing. In part that's because a torrent of foreign currency is needed to finance the trillion dollars worth of goods and services—everything from Japanese cars to Brazilian steel to British oil—that flow between countries each year. In part, it's because corporate money managers have become increasingly sophisticated in searching for the highest, safest yields on their working capital. Every day, tens of billions of dollars worth of currencies are moved from bank to bank and country to country in response to changing market conditions.

Column 1. The country and name of the currency. Note that Ecuador (and many other less-developed countries) shows both an "official" and a "floating" exchange rate.

The first is a rate set by the Ecuadorian government for certain types of transactions within the country. For example, foreign tourists may be legally required to purchase sucres from banks at the official rate. The floating rate is the free market exchange rate that may or may not be legally sanctioned. For example, Ecuadorians investing their savings abroad may be allowed to buy dollars with sucres at the floating rate, but not the lower, official rate.

"SDR" stands for the Special Drawing Rights created by an international organization in Washington called the International Monetary Fund. SDRs aren't currencies in the usual sense. There is no place where you can buy a hamburger or a newspaper with a handful of SDR coins. The SDR is really an index of currency value based on a basket of U.S., German, French, British, and Japanese currencies. The international monetary fund keeps certain accounts in SDRs. And sometimes business contracts are written so that payment can be made in any of the individual currencies in the basket at its current exchange value with SDRs.

"ECU" stands for European Currency Unit. Like the SDR, it is more an index than a currency. The value of an ECU is the weighted average of the value of a bunch of European currencies. ECUs are largely used as a unit of exchange within Europe. Sometimes private contracts are written with prices in ECUs but payable in any major world currency.

Column 2. The number of U.S. dollars it would take to buy a unit of foreign currency that day at 1:00 P.M. in New York. Stock market transactions are usually quoted for the end of the trading day. But dollars are being bought and sold around the clock somewhere in the world. Hence the logic of quoting exchange rates at a time when trading is open in America, but closed in the major currency markets in Europe and Asia.

According to the table, it cost $1.22 to purchase a British pound. That is the price at which banks traded pounds in million-dollar lots. An individual buying a few thousand dollars' worth would have to pay between 2 and 10 percent more.

Note the 30-, 90-, and 180-day "forward" rates quoted for British pounds. A forward rate is the rate at which a currency can be purchased for delivery on some specified date in the future. Forward currency markets exist between the half-dozen currencies used for world trade, and for good reason.

Forward currency contracts are useful for people who have a bill to pay in a foreign currency weeks or months in the future and don't want to take the risk that exchange rates will change in the meantime. Consider an American importer who agrees to pay 16 pounds each for wool sweaters from Britain when they arrive in Houston in 90 days. To lock in the exact number of dollars the sweaters will cost, she buys 90-day forward pounds at a rate of $1.1988 per pound (plus brokerage commissions).

Column 3. The number of dollars it took to buy a unit of foreign currency twenty-four hours earlier. Note that British currency was almost 4 percent cheaper for Americans on Monday than on Tuesday. By historical standards, that is a dramatically rapid shift in rates. But in recent years rapid shifts have become quite common, reflecting both an explosion of speculation in foreign currencies and the unwillingness of governments to inter-

(TABLE 15)
FOREIGN EXCHANGE*

1	2	3
COUNTRY	U.S. $ EQUIVALENT	
	TUES.	MON.
Brazil (Cruzeiro)	.0002024	.0002024
Britain (Pound)	1.2200	1.1820
30-Day Forward	1.2155	1.1773
90-Day Forward	1.2079	1.1698
180-Day Forward	1.1988	1.1602
Ecuador (Sucre)		
Official rate	.01489	.01489
Floating rate	.008849	.008849
SDR	0.979662	0.976173
ECU	0.702132	0.690176

*Transaction information for illustration only.

vene in the currency markets to dampen the shifts in currency values.

Column 4. The number of units of foreign currency it would take to buy a dollar. The information in this column complements the information in column two. But in some cases, it is easier to use. Thus, while it may take a pocket calculator to figure out what a dollar-cruzeiro

4	5
CURRENCY PER U.S. $	
TUES.	MON.
4940.00	4940.00
.8200	.8291
.8827	.8324
.8279	.8378
.8342	.8447
67.18	67.18
113.00	113.00
1.02076	1.02441
. .	. .

exchange value of .0002024 means, the idea of 4940 cruzeiros to the dollar is a snap to comprehend.

Column 5. Exchange rates twenty-four hours earlier, complementing the information in column 3.

PART TWO

The Numbers

Stock Market Indexes

Are stocks up or down? By how much? It's easy to answer the question for any individual stock: if IBM sold for 130 yesterday and 132 today, it must have gone up two dollars a share, or about 1.54 percent. But stock prices change by varying percentages and in different directions. The search for a single number to describe what's happening to the whole market led to the creation of the stock indexes.

The indexes are averages of stock prices, in some cases adjusted for the relative size of the companies included and set at some nice round number for a base year value. The adjustment, or "weighting," is meant to assure that a 1-percent increase in the stock of a company with a market value of $1 billion counts just one-twentieth as much as a 1-percent increase in a $20 billion company. The base year adjustment—say, setting

1990 equal to 100—makes for easy comparisons over time. If, for example, our hypothetical index reached 200 in 2000, it would be obvious that stock prices had doubled over the decade.

Dow Jones Industrial Average. The most frequently quoted index—the one they always flash on the evening news shows—is the Dow Jones Industrial Average. *For all its fame, though, "the Dow" isn't a very useful index.* In part that's because it includes only thirty companies. They may have been representative of industrial America in 1945, but no more. The thirty (beginning with the Allied Signal Corporation, ending with Woolworth) are mostly "smokestack" companies. For example, three chemical companies (Du Pont, 3M, Union Carbide) are included, but only one computer company (IBM).

The Dow can also be misleading because it is not weighted by the relative size of the companies comprising the index. Thus a two point rise in J.P. Morgan or Woolworth stock has the same effect on the index as a two point rise in General Motors or IBM.

Perhaps the reason the Dow is so popular is because it has been around so long. Charles Dow, the publisher of the *Wall Street Journal,* started keeping daily records of the index in 1884. More likely, though, it's because people like big numbers. Somehow it just seems more exciting to speculate about whether the Dow will break 4000 this year than, say, to ponder the probability that the average price of a share will rise 16 percent by December.

Dow Jones Utility Average. The Utility Average covers fifteen big natural gas and electricity utilities. Since the prices of utility stocks used to fluctuate more or less consistently with interest rates, the average was often read as a barometer of what investors thought would happen to rates in the near future. But in recent years factors such as the demand for electric power, the attitudes of regulators, and public hostility to nuclear power have influenced utility prices, too.

Dow Jones Transportation Average. The Transportation Average tracks the fortunes of twenty transport companies. All twenty used to be railroads, but in recent years six airlines and three trucking companies have been substituted for a like number of choo-choo stocks. The most careful followers of the Transportation Index are believers in the Dow Theory. Dow theorists claim that stock prices go up or down in long waves. The tricky part, apparently, is distinguishing short-term movements from the long-term trend.

One clue, the Dowists claim, is whether both the Transportation and the Industrial averages are heading in the same direction. If, for example, the DJIA spurts up but the Transportation Average lingers behind, chances are the market upswing is temporary. However, if both averages enjoy solid gains, it's time to buy.

The trouble with the Dow Theory (and many similar "technical" theories) is that the theorists are a little vague about how much the averages have to change to mark a clear signal of a major market move. *Statistical analysis is sticky stuff. Beware stock market prophets bearing newsletters*.

The Standard and Poor's 500 Index. The S&P 500 has

all the virtues and none of the vices of the Dow. It includes many more common stocks (400 industrial, 40 financial, 20 transportation and 40 utility companies). It is weighted by the total value of shares outstanding, so fluctuations in the stock price of big companies count proportionately more than fluctuations in little ones. And because statisticians have gone to the trouble of grafting it to a much older capitalization-based index, the S&P 500 can be used to compare market averages all the way back to 1893. The Industrial, Financial, Transportation, and Utility components of the S&P 500 are also published separately.

Experts use the S&P 500 as a benchmark of overall market performance. If, for example, your mutual fund did no better over the last decade than this broadbased index, it's pretty clear the fund's managers have not earned their keep.

By the way, several mutual funds, most notably, the Vanguard Index Trust, do not even try to beat the average, but simply to match it. As money is added to the fund, it buys stocks in proportion to their weighting on the S&P 500. *So-called index funds (there are many others available to pension systems, bank trust departments, and other institutional investors) are very popular with business-school types who don't believe that anyone can expect to beat the market for very long.*

The New York Stock Exchange Composite Index. Another broad-based index, this one a value-weighted index of all the companies listed on the New York Stock Exchange. Typically, it tracks the changes in the S&P

500 because the 500 companies in the latter represent a large part of the value of the NYSE Index. Remember, though, only large companies are permitted to join the New York Stock Exchange. So in times when the stocks of smaller companies are particularly hot (or particularly cold), the NYSE may diverge from other indexes.

That, by the way, is where two other value-weighted indexes, the *American Stock Exchange Market Value Index* and the *NASDAQ Over-the-Counter Composite Index,* fit in. The former covers all the stocks on the American Stock Exchange. Since they are, on average, much smaller than the companies on the New York Stock Exchange, this index is a better indicator of what investors think about medium-large (smallish large?) businesses. The NASDAQ index of about 3,500 stocks includes still smaller companies. It tends to be more volatile than the New York or American indexes, because many of the companies traded over the counter are ''go-go'' stocks that operate on a roller coaster of investor optimism and pessimism.

The Wilshire 5000 Index. Looking for the very best index? There is no single best because each measures different things which are important to different people. *However, if ''best'' means broadest based, the easy winner is the Wilshire 5000.* It covers over 5,000 stocks, weighted by capitalization. Most newspapers don't publish it on a daily basis, but you can find it in the *Wall Street Journal* and the *New York Times.*

Interest Rates

Federal Funds Rate. Reported daily in major newspapers, usually as a high, low, and closing rate. This is the interest banks charge each other for one-day loans of $1 million or more. Banks are required to hold a minimum percentage of their assets as currency in the vault, or as no-interest deposits with the Federal Reserve. So at the end of each business day, banks that don't have enough reserves on hand to satisfy the government borrow from those that have an excess. The transfers, totalling tens of billions of dollars each day, are all managed by telex.

Well, you probably aren't in the banking business, and you don't want to borrow $1 million. Why should you care what Citibank charges the Bank of America? *Because the federal funds rate is the single best measure of the current cost of money.*

The federal funds rate is a "pure" interest rate, one

without any premium for the risk of default. A lender incurs no risk since the transaction amounts to an electronic transfer credit between accounts at a government agency. Nothing, moreover, inhibits the fed funds rate from fluctuating rapidly. Thus changes in the rate are a good indicator of what the federal government and other big debtors—and ultimately, you—will have to pay for credit in the coming days and weeks. By the same token, it offers hints about what will happen to the price of bonds and interest-sensitive stocks, such as electric utilities.

Broker Call Loan Rate. Reported daily in major newspapers, this is the rate (or range of rates) stockbrokers charge for loans secured by stocks and bonds in your brokerage account. It tracks changes in the federal funds rate pretty closely because it represents a convenient alternative for banks that would otherwise loan excess reserves to other banks.

The rate is a big higher than the fed funds rate, typically a percentage point higher. But it is still the very cheapest source of credit for individuals. *If you own stocks, use this borrowing privilege before considering a personal loan from a bank or credit card.*

Prime Rate. Reported daily. It is the rate banks say they charge on loans to their very best corporate customers. Often it is also used as a base for calculating rates on other loans. A bank might, for example, set the rate if charges to smaller, less creditworthy businesses as the prime rate plus two percentage points.

In theory, different banks could set their prime rates at different levels and change them as frequently as they like. In practice, big banks in big cities usually match the rates charged by lending lenders, such as Morgan Guaranty, Bank of America, and Manufacturers Hanover. And unlike the federal funds rate, banks rarely adjust their prime more than every month or two. A change can thus be big news, signaling a tightening or loosening of credit in the economy.

A decade ago, the prime was just what banks claimed it was. But today, many banks tell white lies, lending to customers they really want to attract at rates below the prime. The prime has become a bit like the official coach fare posted by airlines. That's the fare airlines charge customers who are least sensitive to cost and least able to shop around. Then it fills the empty seats by charging lower rates to people who would otherwise fly some other airline, or not fly at all.

Foreign Prime Rates. Reported daily in the *Wall Street Journal.* Though not strictly comparable to the American prime rates, the rates printed for Canada, Britain, Germany, Switzerland, and Japan do give a good indication of what it costs big, creditworthy customers to borrow in foreign currencies.

Those rates are sometimes higher, sometimes lower than the American prime. That's because lenders and borrowers who are as at home in one currency as another must factor in a guess about relative movements in exchange rates.

Suppose a Japanese oil refiner needs funds to import crude oil from the Middle East. The refiner could borrow Japanese yen at Japanese interest rates then convert the yen to dollars to pay off the sheiks. Or the refiner could borrow dollars in New York at higher, American interest rates.

Why would the refiner ever borrow the more expensive dollars? Because the refiner may figure that the dollar will depreciate in value sufficiently to compensate for the higher interest rate. If, for example, interest rates were four percentage points higher in dollars, but the dollar depreciated by five percent (relative to yen) over the course of a year when the loan was to be repaid, the Japanese refiner would be better off borrowing in dollars. So national differences in the prime rates are really the market's guess about what will happen to currency exchange rates.

Treasury Bill Rates. Auction results reported weekly; secondary market reported daily in most newspapers. Treasury bills—U.S. government bonds that mature in less than one year—are auctioned every Monday by the Federal Reserve. Once rates are determined competitively, smaller investors are permitted to buy bills at the average rate.

T-bills are sold in $10,000 minimums in "discount" form. The buyer initially pays less than the face value of the bond. The difference, around $250 on a $10,000 bill that matures in 90 days, represents the interest. There is a flourishing "secondary" market for T-bills, with billions' worth traded in each day. So it is always possible to tailor a purchase to a precise number of weeks, or own a bill in a single day. Banks and brokers handle the transactions for fairly modest fees. See page 44 for the details on how to read the numbers for this secondary market.

The T-bill rate is perhaps the most important rate for individual investors to follow. Next to the federal fund rate, it is probably the most sensitive indicator of interest rate trends in the economy. *Most important, it is the yardstick by which money market funds and banks compete for investors' cash.* Thus an increase in the T-bill rate this week will almost certainly translate into a rise in the rates paid by the banks and funds.

The Other Numbers

How're we doing? It may be easy to add up your personal scorecard—earnings, job promotions, and the like. But measuring the performance of the economy and predicting its future is another matter entirely. Here are some of the numbers the experts use in lieu of crystal ball. You'll generally find them in news stories rather than statistical columns.

Output

Gross National Product (GNP). The total value of the finished goods and services produced in the economy. Note the word "finished." *In order to avoid counting output more than once, the GNP doesn't include the value of, say, the wheat that goes into making Wheaties. But it does, of course, include the wheat that is sold abroad as raw wheat.*

GNP is not a precise measure of national economic well-being. But "real" GNP (the GNP adjusted for inflation) may be the closest single number we've got to such a measure. The rate of growth of the GNP is reported every three months by the Commerce Department. Note that GNP growth (and most other rates reported by the government) is "annualized." If, for example, the GNP rose by 1.1 percent in the quarter of a year between March 31 and June 30, the annualized growth rate would be four times 1.1 percent, or 4.4 percent.

When the economy is coming out of a recession, GNP can grow quite quickly, sometimes at an annualized rate as high as 8 or 9 percent. That's because there is plenty of unused economic capacity, and managing rapid growth is only a matter of getting people and machines back to work.

But over the long run, the size of the work force, the quantity of capital, and the rate of productivity change put a ceiling on the growth rate of GNP. Very young economies that are just putting modern production techniques into place—for example, Japan early in this century—have sometimes grown at 10 percent annually for decades. *But mature economies like ours probably couldn't manage more than 4 percent a year for very long.* That is why very rapid growth of GNP creates the fear that inflation is on the way.

Industrial Production. A measure of industrial output is published once a month by the Federal Reserve. Unlike the gross national product, this number is an index in which production is measured by a benchmark of 100 set in 1990. If, for example, the industrial output index were 127 this month, it would mean the rate of output was 27 percent greater than in 1990.

Industrial production includes mining, manufacturing, and energy, but it omits one whopping big chunk of GNP: transportation, services, and agriculture. It is more volatile than GNP: in a modern recession in which GNP slips by 2 or 3 percent, it isn't unusual for industrial production to fall by 10 percent.

Productivity

Capacity Utilization. This number, published monthly by the Federal Reserve, is an estimate of the percentage of factory capacity that is being used. The highest it can possibly be is 100. But capacity utilization rarely exceeds 90 percent, and for good reason. All manufacturing facilities have a rate of output at which production costs are lowest. Above the rate, costs typically go up quickly because workers must be paid overtime, because machines wear out at accelerated speeds, and because there isn't adequate opportunity for the maintenance of equipment.

It may pay a company to exceed this efficient rate of capacity utilization for brief periods in order to fill orders. During World War II, many factories exceeded their efficient production rate for years. *But very high rates of utilization for the economy as a whole—over 85 percent—suggest that inflation is on the way.*

Labor Productivity. Reported quarterly by the Department of Labor, this number is an estimate of the output of the economy divided by the number of work hours it took to produce it.

Interpreting this number is tricky. Compared over decades, labor productivity is a crucial measure of economic success or failure. *If productivity grows rapidly, the chances are excellent that the benefits will be broadly enjoyed in the form of higher wages and higher living standards*. If productivity doesn't grow, the only way the average worker can live better is if (a) he or she puts in longer hours, or (b) a larger percentage of total output is paid in wages rather than interest or profit.

But as the economy cycles from prosperity to recession and back, other factors are at work that make it difficult to interpret productivity changes in the short run. Labor productivity virtually always goes up during recessions because the least efficient workers—and machines—are generally laid off first. For similar reasons, productivity usually falls as business scrambles to put labor and capital back to work.

Many economists would argue, though, that some of the productivity growth during recessions is the healthy result of greater competition for business survival. Under the pressure of falling profits and the threat of lost jobs, labor and management are forced to do their jobs better. This is the closest thing to a plausible rationale for why lean times may lead to fat.

Employment

Unemployment rate. Reported monthly by the Labor Department, this is an estimate of the percentage of people who are unemployed and are actively looking for work. Month-to-month changes of one- or two-tenths of a percentage point, even after adjustments for the seasonal ebb and flow of the supply and demand for labor, don't tell much. A big strike, or simply errors in estimation, may be the cause. So, too, many fluctuations in the number of "discouraged" workers—chronically unemployed workers who give up looking and thus cease to be part of the official statistics. *But larger changes over periods of several months tell a lot about how well the economy is doing and how hard it is to find work.*

The unemployment figures are broken down into groups by race, sex, and age. Unemployment of adult males usually tracks overall economic activity best.

Female unemployment is always higher than male, unemployment of blacks is higher yet, unemployment of black teenagers highest of all (it is not unusual for 40 percent of the last group to be looking in vain for work). In part this is due to racial and sexual discrimination in hiring. But there are other causes, too. Many employers believe that younger workers and female workers are less likely to stay on the job. And there is no question that a higher percentage of young, black, and female workers lack skills and experience.

During recessions, overall unemployment may run as high as 10 or 11 percent. Even in the best of times, millions of people are unemployed. This persistent level of joblessness has led economists to theorize about the "natural" rate of unemployment. When unemployment falls below this rate, employers have trouble matching qualified job seekers to the available work. To get the workers they want, they raise the wages offered. The higher labor costs are then passed on to consumers in the form of higher prices. Higher prices, in turn, lead to demands for still higher wages. The resulting wage-price spiral is only broken when unemployment again rises above the natural rate.

All that may sound reasonable. But why should the unemployment rate at which prices are stable be as high as 4 or 5 percent of the work force?

Conservatives focus on the role of economic incentives: Unemployment compensation, welfare, and high income tax rates make workers choosier about the jobs they are willing to take. Unions, minimum wages, and high social security wage taxes make employers less willing or able to hire workers without experience or proven skills. *Liberals emphasize social factors:* discrimination, rapid shifts in the location of industry, poor schools, and inadequate training programs.

Employment-Population Ratio. Reported monthly by the Labor Department, this is the percentage of the population over age sixteen that is employed. *Quarter-to-quarter changes in this number offer more insight into the "tightness" of the labor market than the unemployment figures because it includes everyone, not just people actively looking for work.* Over longer periods, though, the meaning of trends in the employment-population ratio is muddied by very complicated factors. For example, the reentry of married women into the labor force in the 1970s substantially raised the ratio. And in the future it may be altered by changing attitudes toward retirement.

Average work weeks and average factory overtime. Reported monthly by the Department of Labor. Given the choice, most managers would rather adjust the number of hours workers put in than hire new employees or fire old ones. It's true that overtime is costly: the law requires time-and-a-half pay. But changing the work force is even costlier. New workers must be trained. Firing workers raises the taxes employers must pay into state unemployment compensation funds. And since most managers do have the choice, the average work week and average overtime hours both respond more quickly to the changing demand for labor than do employment figures.

The Money Supply

Each Thursday afternoon after the stock exchanges have closed, an independent government agency called the Federal Reserve releases a long list of financial statistics. They are published the next morning, in some cases in abbreviated form, in most big city newspapers. To the uneducated reader, the weekly Fed statistics are about as interesting (and about as comprehensible) as the Jakarta telephone directory. And twenty years ago hardly anybody except a few professionals bothered to decipher them.

Most economists, including many who believe that long-term trends in the supply of money are useful in predicting interest rates, economic growth, inflation, and stock prices, argue that these weekly statistics don't mean very much. The numbers are too heavily influenced, they say, by extraneous factors.

Nonetheless, Fed watching has become a passion on Wall Street. *If enough people believe the weekly numbers mean the same thing and act on their interpretations, their views can be self-fulfilling.* Here, very briefly, is what they may be thinking.

Money is the grease which allows the wheels of the "real" economy—the factories, shops, farms, etc.—to turn. If there is too little of it, the price of borrowing money goes up. Higher interest rates mean lower prices for bonds and other securities which pay a fixed-dollar return. They also mean less demand for items bought on credit, everything from machine tools to autos to houses. And that means higher costs and less profit for businesses that sell to credit-sensitive customers. *So "tight" money can also lend to lower stock prices.*

Too much money, on the other hand, generates a different set of risks for investors. When banks have more money to lend, interest rates tend to fall. Accordingly, bond and stock prices tend to rise. But that is only the initial effect. Too much money chasing too few goods creates inflation. If the prices of goods and services go up, or if lenders and borrowers expect prices to go up in the near future, interest rates will also go up.

It's easy to see why. If lenders believe they will be paid back in dollars with less purchasing power, they will insist on more interest as compensation. If borrowers believe the same thing, they will be more willing to pay the higher rates. So inflation, or the expectation of inflation, can lead to higher interest rates. And this, in turn, leads to both lower bond and stock prices.

That leaves not one, but two, $64 questions: How do you measure the quantity of money? How much money is not too little and not too much, but jus-s-s-st right?

Everybody knows what money is—the silver and green stuff in your pocket. Along with cash, though, you would certainly want to include the money in your checking account. Now things get trickier. How about bank savings deposits? Shares in money market funds? U.S. Savings Bonds? U.S. Treasury securities that can be turned into cold cash with a phone call to your broker?

The experts don't agree, so the Fed keeps track of several different series of money supply numbers, three of which are published weekly:

M1. The most conservative definition of money. It consists of currency and bank checking deposits held by the public, plus credit union deposits and travelers' checks issued by companies that aren't banks.

M2. A much broader definition to include more assets that can be quickly converted to spendable form. It consists of everything in M1, plus money market fund shares owned by individuals, plus uninsured overnight loans to banks, plus savings accounts, plus bank savings certificates in sums smaller than $100,000. Deposits in retirement accounts are excluded.

M3. A still broader definition. Everything in M2 plus bank savings certificates larger than $100,000, plus uninsured loans to banks that are backed by U.S. Treasury securities, plus dollar deposits in overseas branches of American banks, plus money market fund shares owned by pension funds and other institutions.

A fourth, less-often used definition of money that goes beyond M3 is called L. It consists of M3 plus all other easily measured liquid assets in the economy that could serve the function of money: U.S. Treasury bills, U.S. Savings Bonds, short-term debts of blue-chip corporations (called commercial paper), tradable short-term debts from corporation to banks (called bankers' acceptances), dollar deposits by U.S. residents in European banks (called Eurodollars).

Like all definitions of money, of course, L doesn't quite describe what we want to know because it can't measure the intentions of the people who own the assets.

Now for that second question. *Twenty years ago, most economists would have said the right amount of money was simply the amount that kept interest rates stable. Today, most are fence sitters:* they still believe that money drives the economy through its effect on interest rates. But they accept the idea that the changes in the quantity of money create expectations of inflation and therefore have an independent effect on economic growth and securities prices.

So the Federal Reserve's Open Market Committee— the seven presidentially appointed members of the Federal Reserve Board plus three heads of regional Federal Reserve banks—periodically set targets for growth of each of the money supply aggregates. The target rates are supposed to allow for the creation of enough money to permit the economy to grow without increasing inflationary pressures.

That, of course, only begs the original question. *There is no generally accepted theory of how much money is enough*. In the real world much seems to turn on the market's belief that the people in charge will do whatever is needed, including sacrificing economic growth and employment, to hold the line on prices. When the target rates for money supply growth are exceeded for several weeks in a row, or when the Chairman of the Federal Reserve suggests that inflation may not be so terrible after all, many investors get edgy. *And right or wrong, if they're edgy, maybe you should be, too*.

A last issue of some confusion: Once the Fed sets targets for the money supply numbers, how does it go about hitting them?

The Fed's primary method is "open market" operations. If it wants to increase the supply, it buys government bonds that are owned by the public. The public swaps bonds, which aren't part of the money supply, for Fed-issued cash and checks, which are. If the Fed wants to reduce the money supply, it reverses the process, selling government bonds that it already owns. The public gives up checking deposits, which are part of the money supply, for bonds, which aren't.

It sounds simple; in practice it's pretty messy. Sometimes the Fed tries to increase the money supply, but the independent actions of private lenders and borrowers offset their actions. For the same reasons, the Fed sometimes overshoots. Given enough time, such mistakes can be corrected. But Wall Street remains fixated by the weekly money supply numbers.

Inflation

The Consumer Price Index. Reported monthly by the Labor Department. The concept, if not the execution, is a snap. The government surveys the price of a market basket of goods which is supposed to represent the average consumer's buying habits. It includes everything from T-shirts to T-Birds in rough proportion to the amounts actually purchased. This dollar figure is then adjusted to an index number, based on a value of 100 in 1982. If, for example, the index were 151.6 this month, the goods and services that cost $100 in 1982 cost $151.60 today.

For most purposes, changes in the index are of more interest than the level. They are usually reported as an annualized percentage. If, for example, the index went up by four-tenths of a percent last month, the annualized rate would be twelve times that fraction, of 4.8 percent.

Just to confuse matters, there are two CPIs. The one most commonly cited, the CPI-W, tracks the prices paid by all wage earners and clerical workers. The other, the CPI-U, follows the prices paid by consumers in urban areas. But not to worry: since the two indexes don't diverge all that much, the distinction hardly matters to most of us. The people who may care, though, are workers and retirees whose monthly checks are linked to one index or the other.

Two points to think about. First, the CPI is an average of everybody's prices. *Since you aren't likely to buy the same goods in the same proportion as the average person, the CPI doesn't really reflect your cost of living.* If, for example, you buy a lot of books or drink a lot of wine or fly frequently on airplanes, you've done better than the CPI over the last decade because the prices of these goods and services have lagged behind inflation. On the other hand, if you eat out a lot or rent an apartment rather than own a house, you've done worse.

Second, the CPI is really an overestimate of how much the cost of living has changed for the average person. That's because the index can't take into account quality improvements in existing products or the introduction of new ones.

Don't believe it matters much? Try this experiment. Browse through one of those reproductions of an old turn-of-the-century Sears catalogue. Then ask yourself whether you would rather have $1,000 to spend on the old items at the old prices, or $1,000 to spend at Sears today at current prices. Some of the old products, like simple hand tools, would be a great bargain at the old prices. But the same can't be said for the washing machines or toasters. And the comparison doesn't even make sense for new inventions like stereos or video recorders.

The Producer Price Index. Reported monthly by the Labor Department. The PPI used to be called the Wholesale Price Index, which is what it really is: the price that producers of finished goods charge to their customers. Like other price indexes, it is an estimate of the changes in costs of a "basket" of goods. Like the CPI, it is adjusted to an index level, where prices in 1982 are arbitrarily set at 100.

The PPI is more sensitive to changes in the costs of raw materials and somewhat less sensitive to changes in the cost of labor than the Consumer Price Index. That's because the costs of PPI leaves out—in particular, retailing and advertising—are almost entirely labor costs.

The PPI is particularly interesting because it's a pretty good forecaster of consumer prices to come. *If producer prices are stable, the prices of goods passed on to consumers over the coming months will probably be stable, too.* If not, watch out.

Unit Labor Costs. Reported quarterly by the Department of Labor. This is an index of total output by private firms in the economy, divided by total labor compensation—wages, fringes, and social security. The number is then fitted to an index, with 1987 equal to 100. If, for example, the index were 121.5 today, output that used

$100 worth of labor to make in 1982 now uses $121.50 worth of labor to make.

Actually, trends in this index can be more useful than the level. Over long periods of time, there need not be a fixed relationship between prices in the economy and unit labor costs. Companies might, for example, shift to production processes that use much more or much less labor without greatly affecting the cost of the product. Over a period of a few years, though, the links between labor costs and product costs can be pretty close. *If unit labor costs are rising more rapidly than consumer prices, labor is apparently becoming scarce, and inflationary pressures are building in the economy.* If, on the other hand, unit labor costs are falling behind changes in the overall price level, inflationary pressures are cooling.

Economic Indicators

Corporate Profits. Estimated quarterly by the *Wall Street Journal* and (separately) by the Department of Commerce. The *Journal* surveys the profits of about 500 companies, publishing a report about a month after the quarter ends. The Commerce Department survey, published three weeks later, covers most of corporate America.

Profit, of course, is what's left over after other expenses—taxes, wages, rent, and materials—have been paid. And since business cannot rapidly adjust the size of its labor force or production capacity, profits bear the brunt of ups and downs in the economy. *Thus in a recession in which output falls by 2 percent, profits may drop by 20 percent or more.* What works on the way down also works on the way up: during booms, profits rise much more rapidly than output or total wages.

Profit is also the reward for ownership. The more

companies earn, the more the stock is worth. So you might expect that stock prices would rise (or fall) with news from the quarterly surveys. In fact, the market's response is not so predictable.

Sophisticated investors know about cycles in profitability and take them into account when they decide to buy or sell. But unanticipated quarterly results—profits that are either higher or lower than generally expected—do affect stock prices. Grim news will almost certainly lower stock prices. Very good results will raise stock prices, provided investors do not interpret the news as a harbinger of general inflationary pressure in the economy.

Most economists used to believe that stocks were a good hedge against the value-eroding effects of inflation. As the general price level went up, they argued, the average corporation should be able to maintain its profitability by selling its products for more money. But markets don't run by theories. And, in fact, stocks took a terrible beating during the inflation of the 1970s. Ever since, people have been debating why.

One straightforward explanation is that investors believe that inflation always leads to recession. Thus they anticipate that profits will inevitably fall in real terms when the government responds to inflation by tightening fiscal and monetary policies.

A more complicated hypothesis, one now widely accepted by economists, is that the effective rate of taxation on profits goes up with inflation. In times of rapidly rising prices, the cost of replacing worn-out equipment also rises. But the tax laws treat these costs as an nvarying constant, and thus force companies to pay profits taxes on funds that should properly go to replace depreciated assets. So, the theory goes, more inflation leads to lower real after tax profits, which in turn leads to a lower valuation for stocks.

Got it? Don't worry if you don't. *The important thing to remember is that the stock market is probably a bad place to invest if you expect inflation to heat up*.

Personal Disposable Income. Reported monthly by the Commerce Department. Take the sum of private earnings—wages, salaries, pensions, dividends, interest, and rent. Add government "transfer payments," such as unemployment insurance, social security benefits, welfare, and veterans' benefits. Then subtract taxes paid by individuals, including social security deductions. What's left is a measure of personal spending power, what individuals have to divide between consumption and savings.

PDI (and its change from previous months) is interesting for a bunch of reasons. *To begin, it is one good, bottom-line measure of how well or poorly we are doing as a group*. Other statistics, such as GNP, are at least one step removed from personal spending power. Personal income never falls as far or as fast as national output during a recession. That's because the federal government acts as a buffer, collecting less taxes and paying out more in benefits.

For stock market watchers, personal income is a good indicator of the ability of the public to buy autos, appliances, air travel, and other goods whose purchase can be postponed. *A flat or falling PDI is thus bad news for these highly cyclical industries*. Remember, though, rising personal income does not guarantee rising purchases. If people have badly depleted their savings during a recession or simply fear that another downturn is on the way, they may be reluctant to spend.

Inventories. Reported monthly by the Department of Commerce. Inventories are supplies, products in the process of being manufactured, and unfinished goods yet to be sold by businesses. The drums of paint waiting to cover Chevy Luminas at a General Motors plant represent inventory. So do the tape cassette decks ready to be installed in the Luminas, and the thousands of Luminas already in transit to dealers. So, too, for that matter, is the spare roll of paper towels in the executive washroom at the Lumina plant.

From a company's perspective, the choice of how much inventory to carry is often a critical and difficult decision. A lot of inventory reduces the possibility you'll run out of supplies or finished product in periods of unanticipated demand. But, by the same token, it costs money to carry inventory—money to carry the investment in supplies, money to maintain storage facilities, and month to insure their contents.

Japanese factories make a fetish of carrying a bare minimum of inventories. In some, supplies of critical assembly parts are designed to last just a few hours. Suppliers, located within a few miles, are expected to replenish parts several times a day. Nothing comparable is possible in the U.S. because supplies must be shipped great distances, often in unreliable weather. But there is

tle question that the Japanese example, plus a decade
 very high interest rates, has led many American
mpanies to work harder at paring inventories.

*For the economy-watcher, monthly inventory figures
er valuable clues about the direction of output.* As the
onomy moves smartly out of recession, the growth in
les outpaces inventories; thus inventories measured as a
rcentage of monthly sales begin to shrink. So very low
ventory figures suggest the economy is taking off, or at
ry least, ready to grow because sales are outpacing
mand. By similar logic, growth in inventories relative
 sales is a warning that the economy is poised for
cession.

Orders for Nondefense Capital Goods. Reported monthly
 the Commerce Department. Capital goods consist of
dustrial products used to make other products. Some
vel of spending on capital goods is need simply to
place worn-out or obsolete machinery. Some is always
eded to take advantage of new cost-cutting technology
 for the manufacture of new products. But orders for
pital goods are largely dependent on what business
nks sales will be in the future.

That makes outstanding orders for capital goods a
eful barometer for the business cycle. Orders usually
 far behind recovery from a recession. For one thing,
sinesses doubt the recovery will last; for another, they
ually begin an upswing with plenty of unused capacity.
t since there is often a long wait between an order for
uipment and its delivery, companies must eventually
mmit themselves to purchases or risk losing business.

*High and continuing demand for capital goods is thu[s]
a good indication from the people who know best that
recovery is strong.* On the other hand, weak deman[d]
suggests that the recovery may be limited and short-lived[.]

Orders for Machine Tools. Reported monthly by th[e]
National Machine Tool Dealers Association. Machin[e]
tools are machines that shape parts. A few decades ag[o]
most were interchangeable in many plants and processes—
simple drill presses, lathes, plastic extruding machine[s,]
etc. Today, many are specialized hi-tech wonders th[at]
perform dozens of operations in sequence without huma[n]
intervention.

Machine tools are a sub-category of capital good[s.]
Thus it shouldn't be surprising that the two categori[es]
follow similar cyclical patterns. *What makes machin[e]
tools special is that the swings in demand are far mo[re]
dramatic.* When companies that make capital goods a[re]
convinced that business is on the rise, machine to[ol]
orders may double in a matter of months. Collapses i[n]
sales can be just as dramatic.

Index of Leading Indicators. Reported monthly by th[e]
Commerce Department. All sorts of statistics provid[e]
hints about what will happen to the level of econom[ic]
activity over the next few months. But none is consistent[ly]
accurate, and business economists fiercely dispute th[e]
pros and cons of each. What to do?

*The Commerce Department's answer is the practic[al]
equivalent of delegating responsibility to a committe[e.]*
Instead of picking one statistic, they offer an ind[ex]

constructed from twelve different statistics. Components of the index are:

- The money supply (the Federal Reserve's broad M2 definition)
- Outstanding loans to business and consumers
- An index of raw materials prices
- Stock market prices (the Standard and Poor 500 index)
- Business inventories
- Orders for new plant and equipment
- Building permits for new housing
- Incorporations of new businesses
- Companies experiencing delays in receiving orders from suppliers
- Average work week for manufacturing labor
- New orders for consumer goods
- New claims for unemployment insurance

Some of these statistics are measured in dollars, some in hours, and some as index numbers. The index of leading indicators assigns each component an equal weight, then arbitrarily sets 1982 equal to 100. Thus, if the index of leading indicators is 193 this month, it is 93 percent higher than it was in 1982.

Confused? You are not alone. The harder you stare at this index, the less it seems to mean. Probably the best way to use it is to look at the separate components. *If all of them, or almost all of them, are moving in the same direction, there is an excellent chance the economy will follow.* And the more months in a row they all move together and in the same direction, the more confidently one can assume they are right. On the other hand, if some are moving up and some are moving down, or if the index is bumping around from month to month, assume nobody knows what is happening.

International Finance

Merchandise Trade Balance. Reported monthly by the Commerce Department. Add up the dollars foreigners spend here for American goods. Then subtract the dollars Americans spend abroad on foreign goods. The difference is called the "merchandise trade balance."

If America exported $30 billion worth of corn and airplanes and chemicals last month and imported $25 billion worth of cars and cameras and oil, there would be a surplus in merchandise trade of $5 billion.

Such a surplus, by the way, would be quite unusual. Typically, the United States imports more goods than it exports, and is thus in deficit on merchandise trade. That's not necessarily bad: most countries go through long cycles of deficit and surplus that reflect both the costs of production and the purchasing power of investors and consumers. *What is bad, though, is a rapid change in the merchandise trade balance that reflects the collapse of specific industries.*

In the late 1970s the American steel, auto, and consumer electronics industries were all hit hard by import competition. In the early 1980s, the big losers included manufacturers of shoes and inexpensive clothing, and grain farmers. Workers lost their jobs. Suppliers lost business. Stock prices fell. Whole communities dependent on a few large employers were decimated.

It usually pays to avoid investments in companies that have lost their ability to compete in world markets. The profitability of such companies depends on the ability to get the government to protect them against imports. Once they get it, few ever manage to make it on their own again. And historically, few have even managed to prosper while on the government dole.

Current Account Balance. Reported quarterly by the Commerce Department. This one's a bit awkward to explain but worth the trouble to understand. *The current account is the international flow of money for purposes other than investment.* Merchandise trade, discussed above, is one big component. But it also includes (a) the sale and purchase of services, such as tourism, insurance, and banking; (b) interest paid and received on loans; (c) payments of dividends and profits to foreign stockholders; (d) government foreign aid; and (e) gifts to individuals— for example, the money immigrants send to relatives in the old country.

The current account offers a broad picture of how an economy is managing its current finances with the rest of the world. If an economy's current account is in surplus—that is, if foreigners are sending more cash to pay for goods, services, interest, gifts, etc., than they are getting back—the economy is gradually accumulating IOU's from the rest of the world. On the other hand, if an economy's current account is in deficit, the country is living above its means and is gradually becoming indebted to the world. *Unless there is some mitigating circumstance, then, chronic current account deficits are bad news.* They can't go on forever. Eventually, a deficit country must reverse the flows, and typically, that means reducing its living standard.

Capital Account Balance. Reported quarterly by the Commerce Department. Add up all the money foreigners invest in America, everything from the purchase of U.S. Treasury bonds, to farmland in Iowa, to mutual fund shares. Subtract all the money Americans invest abroad. The resulting number is the "capital account balance."

Usually this number is broken down into short-term and long-term capital flows. Short-term capital is cash invested in bank accounts and other places where it can be withdrawn in a matter of hours or days without paying high commissions or penalties. Long-term capital is money locked into stocks or bonds, or the direct purchase of assets such as buildings or even whole companies.

The distinction is important because short-term capital moves restlessly from country to country in search of the highest interest rate or in speculation of a windfall gain associated with changes in exchange rates between currencies. *On the other hand, long-term capital movements usually reflect the work of more fundamental forces, such as the opportunity for profit from the operation of businesses.*

Notice that a surplus on our capital account would mean that foreigners invested more here than we did over there. Such a surplus is the mirror image of a deficit on the current account. When America's capital account is in deficit, people and companies abroad are accepting more dollars from Americans than they are sending back to pay for their purchases here. Those extra dollars, whether they sit around in the form of checking deposits at the Bank of America or are used to purchase IBM stock, represent investments in the United States.

If the foreigners were reluctant to hold these extra dollars in American investments, something would have to give. "Something," in this case, would be the exchange rate between dollars and foreign currencies. Americans who tried to buy things abroad would find they would have to pay more dollars to obtain the same terms. On the other hand, if foreigners were particularly eager to hold their savings in the form of dollars, Americans would find that foreign goods were cheap to buy.

All clear? Don't worry if it's still a little blurry around the edges. Even the pros take months to learn the jargon by heart. Just keep HOW TO READ THE FINANCIAL PAGES nearby for easy reference.

About the Author

PETER PASSELL is the author of the highly acclaimed books *Where to Put Your Money* and *Personalized Money Strategies*. Currently an economics columnist for the *New York Times*, he has been published in numerous magazines and has explained the intricacies of finance on many radio and television shows including *Latenight America*, *Larry King*, and *Independent Network News*. Holder of a Ph.D. in economics from Yale University, he is a former Professor at Columbia University.